CRIMINAL
SELF-CONCEPTIONS IN THE
PENAL COMMUNITY OF
FEMALE OFFENDERS: AN
EMPIRICAL STUDY
MARION R. EARNEST

San Francisco, California
1978

Published By

R & E RESEARCH ASSOCIATES, INC.
4843 Mission Street, San Francisco, California   94112

Publishers

Robert D. Reed and Adam S. Eterovich

Library of Congress Card Catalog Number

77-90378

I.S.B.N.

0-88247-511-8

ACKNOWLEDGMENTS

My appreciation is extended to Dr. Robert G. Caldwell whose continued support, counsel, and guidance has been a most rewarding part of the writer's work.

To the late Dr. Manford H. Kuhn a recognition for his insights, support and suggestions in the early part of this project.

An appreciation to Donald E. Miller's early support and suggestions on the theoretical part of this work.

I am deeply indebted to the women included in this research who were confined in the Wisconsin Home for Women and who served as research subjects for this study. To these unnamed volunteers, this study is dedicated.

In addition, my indebtedness to Mrs. Marcia Simpson, Superintendent; Mrs. Bott, Social Work Supervisor, and the staff who aided in the collection of the data. I am grateful to the Division of Corrections of the State of Wisconsin for their permission, cooperation, and use of data gathered from the correctional facility.

I also recognize a debt to many others: persons who have facilitated this study, as to many colleagues and friends.

To my wife whose patience exceeded that of job, whose aid and sacrifice are not measurable, I owe more than words can express.

TABLE OF CONTENTS

IV FINDINGS (Continued)

V SUMMARY AND CONCLUSION   69

LIST OF TABLES

CHAPTER I

INTRODUCTION

Background of the Problem to be Investigated

Criminologists and sociologists have indicated a growing concern over the obvious neglect of research and study of female offenders as a criminal population (Reckless, 1967:148), (Giallombardo, 1966:2), (Ward and Kassebaum, 1965:V-X). In more recent years Knudten (1970:176-186), Haskell and Yablonsky (1970:60-64), have cited significant contributions to the study of female criminality. Numerous studies relating to female criminality in the specific area of sex offenses are too limited in their approach (sensational exposés) and too narrow in scope to apply to the problem presented for investigation in this study (Giallombardo, 1966:2, 18). The purpose of this study is the identification of a criminal self-conception and the perception of self, as held by female inmates in a penal community.

An early work on the female criminal was completed by Cesare Lombroso, the Italian physician and anthropologist. He found that the majority of female criminals are: (1) less likely to be a "born criminal type" than a male criminal, but (2) more likely to exhibit the characteristics of an occasional criminal (1916).

Perhaps the next important study of female crime is the systematic study of motives by W. I. Thomas in 1923, who viewed the sexually delinquent girl as an unadjusted girl, who uses sex as the means of achieving her four dominant wishes: new experience, recognition, response, and security. In

1

the application of this theory Thomas was able to point out several relationships between these wishes and delinquent behavior (1923:1-69).

In 1934 the Gluecks, in a rather intensive research of 500 consecutive commitments to the Massachusetts Reformatory for Women found five factors
closely associated to non-recidivism: steadiness of employment, economic
responsibility, neighborhood influence within a year of commitment, lack of
retardation in school, and lack of abnormal mental condition. These five
factors were used in the development of a scale to predict those who would be
least likely to return to the institution (1934:288).

One systematic consideration is Pollak's (1950) development of his
"masked" behavior theory of the female offender from his evaluation of criminal
offense records. He points out that criminal records show under-reporting of
female offenses; therefore, the real measure of female criminality must be
sought from unofficial sources (1950:1-7).

More recently Barbara Ann Kay (1961, doctoral dissertation) studied
several components of the self, specifically the direction of socialization,
the amount of alienation, and self-perception as held by 92 per cent of the
324 female offenders in the Ohio Reformatory for Women. On a limited scale,
the above study demonstrated that self-conceptions are related to total arrests,
length of incarceration, and age of onset of illegal behavior. Her principal
findings (Kay, 1961:45-48) were: (1) Female offenders were less negative in
socialization and more alienated than male offenders, (2) factors which motivate
the individual to crime, whatever they are, appear to work earlier on males
than on females, and (3) using the internalization of norms and feelings of
identity with society as components of internal containment, on the socialization and alienation measures, the female and male prisoners showed

2

significant differences in internal containment. She concluded that the social structure (the external containment around the individual) was seemingly able to control females and not let them become involved in delinquency so often or so early as males.

The Kay study was the only work found concerned with the concept of self as it might be applied to female offenders, the area with which the present study will be involved. However, Kay realizes several shortcomings in her study:

> Many aspects of self-conception theory have not been tested in the present research . . . . Further study of self concepts, . . . would probably provide more statistically reliable and valid tests . . . [with] the addition of more discriminating items (1961:46).

It should also be noted that a theoretical orientation was neither developed nor tested, and the inmate's criminal self-conception was not investigated.

Problem to be Investigated

This research is directed toward the social psychological aspect of criminal self-conception in females. It is designed to gather evidence bearing upon some of the theoretical propositions in self-reference group theory. An attempt will be made to explore and explain the presence or absence of criminal self-conception among adult female offenders in a state institution. In other words, this is an empirical study of self-attitudes of women in a penal setting, and should add further insight and knowledge to an area where relatively little is known.

This dissertation project is an adaptation of the William Nardini study (1958, doctoral dissertation), insofar as the conceptualization of the theory, type of hypotheses, and the instrument developed is concerned. Since this study is focused on females rather than males, the Nardini questionnaire has been modified accordingly (Appendix A). The modified questionnaire was pretested on a selected group of 29 inmates at The Women's Reformatory at Rockwell City, Iowa.

The orientation utilized is, an individual's self development socially and symbolically. The theoretical model stems from the writings and contributions of Baldwin, Cooley, Mead, Newcomb, Sherif, Kuhn (1956:3-49) and more recently from Rose (1962) and others.

Reasons for the Study

The decision to study the criminal self-conception of the female inmate was based on the need for information on women offenders, supplemented by the earlier project in which Nardini empirically studied the male first-time offenders' criminal self-conception. The present study was predicated on the assumption that similar hypotheses tested on a female population could be as important in the contribution to knowledge on female offenders as the Nardini study was for males.

In comparison to the male, the female criminal has received much less attention in the area of research. Pollak states:

> The criminality of women is a neglected field of research. Our mental picture of the criminal is that of the male violator of the law, and criminological research seems to have been largely under the spell of this cultural stereotype (Pollak, 1950:XV).

Perhaps the lack of research prior to 1950 is due to the obvious, that is --
a considerably smaller number of women come into contact with the law, police,
courts, and penal institutions than do men. Women comprise over half of our
population. However, they live under conditions, such as dual standards, that
may actually protect them from detection and final prosecution of criminal
acts. The logical reasoning behind this statement is the deferential treatment given the female by the victim, arresting officer, judge or jury, whichever the case may be. Society protects the female through the male. The role
of the male originates in the stereotype of the female as defenseless (Schur,
1969:42). Thus it seems more likely that the female has a better chance of
escaping the criminal label than has the male.

Certainly one of the historical features of our time is women's
progress toward attaining social equality with men. In times of great stress,
such as World War II, women have had to assume numerous roles which are
usually open to men alone. In this context women have, in a qualified sense,
gained equal rights with men. They have continued to be wage earners and in
some instances household heads, but they also have continued to be homemaker,
mother and rearer of offspring, shopper, servant, and nurse for the family
plus all the social roles they had before (Pollak, 1950:154-155). More
recently Bertha J. Payak (1963:7) states, ". . . can only be understood in
the context of her social role." This is in agreement with Pollak's finding
above.

According to Pollak (1950:155), women have been given new opportuni-
ties for crime which they did not have formerly, and figures on criminality
seem to indicate that crimes against property by women have increased. He
also points out that if this newfound freedom were a true expression of social

5

equalization of the sexes one would have to make a further assumption, i.e., a corresponding decrease in the amount of undiscovered female crime. (This might be due to the lag in social expectations.) However, cultural analysis contradicts the validity of this assumption because, as pointed out above, the new roles of women have not replaced the old roles but have become additional roles, thus creating role conflicts. "In other words, they have retained all those roles which account for the amount, the nature, and particularly the masked character of their traditional criminal behavior" (Pollak, 1950:155).

According to Cressey (1970:126-131), the status of sex is the most important single trait significant in differentiating criminals from non-criminals. The essence of this point is indicated when he states:

> In the United States at present, the rate of arrest of males is about eight times the rate of arrest for females; about fifteen times as many males as females are committed to correctional institutions of all kinds; and about twenty times as many males as females are committed to state and federal prisons and reformatories housing serious offenders. (126)

Recent statistical data released by the Attorney General on penal institutions report: (1) At the close of 1966 there were 6,304 female prisoners in Federal and State institutions. (2) Female prisoners comprise 3.2 per cent of the total 199,654 inmates confined to all penal institutions. (3) There was no percentage or ratio difference between State or Federal population (National Prisoner Statistics, 1968).

According to Haskell and Yablonsky (1970:60) low female arrest rates may be partially explained by the failure of their victims to report such offenses. Further, if all female offenses were reported, female rates might more closely approach male rates (1970:60).

6

Knudten (1970:176) has noted that offenses for 1968 reveal: "Female criminality reaches its highest volume in the crimes of drunkeness and larceny. Prostitution and commercialized vice and runaways, disorderly conduct constitute secondary female crime categories." While the Uniform Crime Reports (1970:25) in 1969 state, ". . . females comprised 26 per cent of all arrests for larceny-theft and had a higher involvement in this offense than for any of the index offenses." In other words, women were arrested more frequently for larceny than any other type of offense in 1969. One possible explanation for the increased arrest for women is offered by Haskell and Yablonsky:

> As women increasingly assume the role of breadwinner, they have greater responsibility for providing money for necessities and luxuries, and may more often resort to illegal means of obtaining money when legal means are not available. This may account for the increase in property offenses committed by women. The large number of arrests for drunkeness and the tremendous increase in arrests for violations of narcotic laws (516.7 per cent from 1960 to 1969 [Uniform Crime Reports 1970:111]) may reflect an increase in frustrations experienced by women (1970:64).

To summarize, the available data indicate that females still have a lower crime rate than males; however, the need for research on female criminality is apparent.

Crime and the Criminal Defined

It should be made explicit that this investigator is an advocate of the legal position which holds that ". . . crime is an intentional act or violation of the criminal law (statutory and case law), committed without defense or excuse, and penalized by the state as a felony or misdemeanor" (Tappan, 1947:100). One exception to this definition is involuntary manslaughter.

7

The unconvicted and suspect cannot be known as a violator of the law; to assume his so would be in derogation of our most basic political and ethical philosophies. In empirical research it would be quite inaccurate, obviously, to study all suspects or defendants as criminals (Tappan, 1947:100).

Caldwell further states, a violation of a group norm is not to be labeled criminal until action is taken by our legislative bodies and courts (1956:112-117).

Summary and Conclusion

A review of the literature on the criminality of women indicates a necessary concern, as the crime rate for females has increased. The apparent need for further research, supplemented by the writer's interest in the area, stimulated the present study. Crime and the criminal, as defined from the legalistic view, serve as a general guide for the study.

CHAPTER II

THEORETICAL ORIENTATION

Introduction

The purpose and function of this chapter is to examine, develop, and
present the theoretical orientation that guides this study.

Criminal behavior is viewed as human behavior, therefore, any theory
of criminality should also explain "normal" human behavior. Since crime is a
social phenomenon and there is little evidence to support the biological or
physiological explanations of crime, it seems practical to assume that our
attention should be directed toward the social level, or symbolic language
level to explain criminality. D. R. Cressey supports this view as he writes:

> Criminal behavior is human behavior, has much in common
> with noncriminal behavior, and must be explained within the
> same general framework used to explain other human behavior.
> However, an explanation of criminal behavior should be a
> specific part of a general theory of behavior. Its specific
> task should be to differentiate criminal from noncriminal
> behavior (1970:73).

A brief review of current theories of human behavior will be helpful in developing the theoretical orientation employed in this project.

Theories of Human Behavior

A number of theoreticians have advanced various theories to explain
human behavior, often quite diverse in nature and contradictory in many basic

assumptions involved. The earlier ones are of a psychological nature only and the later ones tend more towards socialization, i.e., a social inter-action approach. Of the several theories to be advanced in the last fifty years probably the most significant are: Freudian theory, field theory, symbolic interaction theory, and reference-group theory; the latter being the basis for the approach taken in this investigation.

Freudian Theory

No doubt Freudian theory has been the most popular and best known of those mentioned above. It is also known as a psychoanalytical theory, which views personality development in terms of the person's inner emotional urges. It places stress upon deviations in the process by which the infant or child passes from his own physical reactions to one of a sense of social responsibility. Freud perceived personality as developing from the Id, the original basic nature of man, to the Ego, the consciousness of man, which attempts to preserve the individual and control the Id which remains un-socialized. The Super-ego develops as the last part of the personality form-ing the conscience and representing, to a large extent, the unconscious morality of man (Caldwell, 1956:186). According to Freud, personality is the set of reciprocal urging and checking of energy forces; however, it is not what it appears to be since a rationalization can be given for the real motives. This rationalization tends to hide meaningful behavior so that even the individual is unconscious of his real motives.

Field Theory

Another important approach to human behavior is field theory, which uses the principles found in Gestalt psychology and applies them to man. The field theorists view human behavior as a function of man's environmental field. Interaction with other people does not influence his behavior; instead, he is pulled and/or pushed by vectors and goals within the field. The individual is, in effect, motivated externally while inner motivation is discounted. This model contrasts completely with the Freudian school, which holds that the individual acts from within and not from external fields of force.

Learning Theory

The learning theorists, on the other hand, advocate the Stimulus-response (S-R) model as propounded by the Pavlovian and Watsonian School and known as "behaviorism" in the 1920's. The Clark Hull learning theory is an extention of the earlier S-R school. Hull's model is largely a biological approach to human behavior; it assumes that the neurological system remains quiescent unless activated by outside stimuli. In other words, the individual is neither autonomous nor self-activated, but "kicked" automatically into action by external stimuli (Hickman and Kuhn, 1956:16). In group life the individual is considered as not interacting socially with others, since the socialization process, through which all humans pass, is ignored by such learning theories.

The above three theories give a very brief coverage of the major psychological models of human behavior. However, they gradually became less central to the sociologist with the shift towards socialization and the social interaction approach. Some sociologists refer to this change as the "Chicago tradition" since a majority of the early contributors to the symbolic inter-action theory were associated with the University of Chicago School of

Social Psychology in the early 1900's (Rose, 1962:3) (Miller, M. A. Thesis, 1957:3).

Symbolic Interaction Theory

The symbolic interactionist approach in the area of social-psychology rests almost entirely on propositions and assumptions concerning the purely social and cultural nature of human behavior, rather than on the physiological and neurological determinants sociologists utilized previous to this time. The symbolic interaction approach was innovated by William James and James Mark Baldwin and developed in various ways by G. H. Mead, C. H. Cooley, E. Faris, and H. Blumer, et al. The symbolic interactionists place central importance on language as a process in man's socialization. This approach contends that man learns about himself by internalizing those views he shares with groups via language. Within this social-psychological frame of reference has developed the model of self-reference groups which is basic to current reference-group theory (Shibutani, 1955).

Reference-Group Theory

The term reference group was first coined by Hyman (1942). It has been employed to explain the most basic kind of social process. The self-reference group concept holds that the individual comes to perceive himself as a certain kind of being as he uses language symbols to define himself apart from all other social objects. Newcomb in his definition of reference group calls attention to others: ". . . a person's attitudes [that] are influenced by a set of norms which he assumes that he shares with other individuals, [and] those individuals constitute for him a reference group" (1950:225).

Briefly, reference groups serve as referents in defining the self and the social world. Reference-group theory constitutes an important basis for self-identity, for the formation and function of the individual's attitudes directing his behavior.

Another form of self-theory, the client-centered theory (Rogers, 1951) with emphasis on self-psychology, has developed more recently (Caldwell, 1965).[1]

Since man is complex and difficult to fathom, his behavior cannot be explained by any one theory. Generally, self-theory contends that human behavior is meaningful, and also structured and consistent. Its correlates are symbols and social reference points which are necessary for meaningful behavior. Man is the only animal that defines and is defined by language. He alone has a "true" language through which abstract meanings can be shared. The individual acts on the basis of his perception, selection, and definition of "reality" in the social world. Therefore, language is essential to the study of meaningful human behavior. It would be difficult, if not impossible, to play or take roles and relate social experience without language. In other words, self-reference group theory is contingent on language. The salient dimensions are self, other social objects, and reference-groups.

The _self_ is viewed as the only object common to all the varied situations in which an individual participates. Through language the self is created and developed by those attitudes the individual holds toward himself as an object within the social process. Thus, self is perceived as a social object. The reciprocal of self is _other social objects_, or all the various social objects except self, which exist in the individual's social world.

13

Certain of these social objects, or _others_, tend to contribute toward anchoring points as they become internalized in the individual's self-conception (Hickman and Kuhn, 1956:43).

The fact that man does not live in isolation, but must live with others, points to the crucial part played by certain others in his behavior. In order to understand man's behavior it is first necessary to recognize the social groups to which he belongs. Groups guide the individual by giving him meanings, values, and attitudes which are then used in developing a definition of his situation. W. I. Thomas has emphasized that the individual defines, then acts according to his definition. These special groups through which man develops attitudes toward himself as a social object are called reference-groups. As the individual internalizes the value system of the group, it then influences his self-attitudes and resulting behavior. The individual is thereby anchored in groups which lend stability as well as meanings and values in an uncertain social world. _Significant others_ represent salient points within groups: they are the anchoring points for the individual; they are crucial to the formation of his self-conception; they are forces of control and influence in the individual for they represent the embodiment of social norms and values (Shibutani, 1961).

Reference groups are defined by the self-theorists as ". . . the groups with which we feel self-identified . . ." (Hickman and Kuhn, 1956:43). According to Newcomb it is possible for a group to be either positive and/or negative as a reference group for one individual, since one may willingly conform to some of its norms but not to others.

A positive reference group is one in which a person is motivated to be accepted and treated as a member (overtly and symbolically), whereas a negative reference group is one which

he is motivated to oppose, or in which he does not want
to be treated as a member" (1950:226).

Individuals probably have more than one reference group; also, these various
reference groups may have different degrees of force or intensity in their
influence upon an individual.

A reference group, as a membership group, differs from the informal
group; it is organized, comprised of official members, and is reputedly
known by its formal membership requirements and the collective membership.
An individual's reference groups are usually his membership groups, but his
membership groups are not necessarily his reference groups.

A reference group influences the individual's self-conception through
what has been called the reference category (Hickman, Kuhn, 1956:43-44).
Social objects are classified into categories. A category becomes a reference
category as it is employed, by those whose opinions are valued for defining
and evaluating the individual. The norms and values of the group are brought
to bear on the individual through the reference category. In other words,
the individual must constantly respond to the judgments of those significant
others who form his reference group.

A reference group may be either positive or negative, depending
upon the individual's perception of it and how he allows it to (directly, or
indirectly) influence his attitudes and, consequently, his behavior. The
individual's perception of the expectations in his reference group may differ
from the motivation (toward as positive; or to oppose as negative) of persons
in the reference group. One might question whether if usually the individual
who perceives that his significant others hold a derogatory reference to him
is motivated to oppose this group.

15

Self-reference group theory, developed from the symbolic interactionist approach, views man in a symbolic environment comprised of systems
of interpersonal networks formed by communication. Thus, man acquires his
"human" qualities directly through association and interaction with others,
and indirectly through language. Therefore, it is not surprising to find
that other social objects, or others as groups become salient factors for
him. Thus, as he comes to perceive himself as a social object, he orients
himself toward his fellow men.

Within this theoretical frame of the self-reference group (its
aspects: self, others, and reference groups) the conceptual dimensions of
this study are later developed.

Critique of Self-Reference Group Theory

Certainly, as in any theory of human behavior, self-reference group
theory has been questioned by authorities in the field. A major criticism
is the lack of empirical evidence to support and substantiate this theoretical approach. Man is highly complex and our knowledge is meager as to how
his ideas and attitudes influence his behavior in the social interaction
process. Professor Caldwell contends that an important weakness of the theory
is implicit in the assumption that the individual knows and is willing and
able to recognize the facts. He notes also that much of personality is
covert or unconscious (1956). In other words, what a person reports about
himself is likely to be distorted by "mechanisms of self-deception," which
serve the purpose of deceiving the individual with respect to his own
motives or intentions. Furthermore, the person often does not know the
"truth" about himself, and he may be reluctant to communicate the facts he
does know.

Another criticism lies in the assumption that as man moves through time the causes of immediate behavior are undoubtedly rooted in the past and influenced by precedents; therefore, a previous condition might unconsciously precipitate present behavior. With the passage of time the powers of memory, recall and perception are dulled. Also, since personality continues to develop, its measurement might show considerable variations throughout the life time of an individual. Self-theorists generally propose that personality is an ongoing process, but herein lies a problem: assuming an individual has some separate identity apart from the group, how may such aspects of personality be studied without being viewed as mere reflections of the group (Wrong, 1961:183-193)?

Another criticism is that self-reference group theory does not adequately explain the learning process. While it emphasizes that an individual internalizes the expectations of the group through the roles that he plays, it does not tell us how he does so. This raises the question - does he learn entirely from his interaction with others, e.g., reference groups, or can he have an entity separate from the group? At this point motivation becomes an important consideration. Self-theory holds that the individual is group motivated but it fails to show why and how this motivation takes place (Caldwell, 1965:199-200). Learning theory that features the individual organism or the psychological structure of the individual has obvious advantages since they represent more direct approaches to both questions how and why.

In order to be scientific, a researcher must be critical of his own theoretical frame of reference. The above criticisms, raised by other researchers, show the need for clarification of the concepts of self-theory and the refinement of present instruments to more accurately measure not only attitudes but also a change in attitudes. Nevertheless, this writer believes that the self-reference group theory is a most promising approach to the study of criminal attitudes of female inmates. Therefore, the self-reference group theory will be the theoretical frame of reference used in this study. The major concepts are self and reference groups.

In conclusion, the reader should be cautioned that this model is not necessarily the only theoretical approach to criminality but rather the one used in this study.

Criminological Theory Restated and Reformulated

Several criminologists, including E. H. Sutherland, W. C. Reckless, and D. G. Glaser have advocated a criminological theory which incorporates several assumptions that have become central in self-theory. As early as 1939 Sutherland made the first application of social psychological theory to criminal behavior. He strongly supported the premise that social interaction between the individual and criminal groups was the major source of criminality. He labeled his orientation, "differential association theory." Sutherland's formulation of causative factors in crime attempts to find a model that would be applicable to white collar criminals as well as hardened underworld criminals (1939:4-9). His theory states that "systematic criminal behavior" is acquired and assimilated through the identical social processes as "systematic lawful behavior." Sutherland proposed that criminal behavior results when an individual's associations are located in criminal groups rather than in lawful groups, and the chances that criminal behavior will be developed is conditioned by the frequency, consistency, and duration (time span) of the individual's exposure with criminal group patterns. In other words, criminal behavior arises basically from the influence of contact with criminal groups.

More specifically, Sutherland's theory extended the following postulates:

1. Criminal behavior is learned.

2. Criminal behavior is learned in interaction with other persons in a process of communication.

3. The principal part of learning of criminal behavior occurs within intimate personal groups.

4. When criminal behavior is learned, the learning includes:

   a. techniques of committing the crime, which are sometimes very simple, sometimes very complicated;

   b. the specific direction of motives, drives, rationalizations, and attitudes.

5. The specific direction of motives and drives is learned from definitions of the legal codes as favorable or unfavorable.

6. A person becomes delinquent because of an excess of definitions favorable to violation of law over definitions unfavorable to violation of law.

7. Differential association may vary in frequency, duration, priority, and intensity.

8. The process of learning criminal behavior by association with criminal and anti-criminal patterns involves all of the mechanisms that are involved in any other learning.

9. While criminal behavior is an expression of general needs and values, it is not explained by those general needs and values since non-criminal behavior is an expression of the same needs and values (Sutherland, 1955:77-80).

It becomes apparent that one finds some similarity between Sutherland's "differential association theory" and contemporary self-reference group theory, for Sutherland's basic assumption is that an individual becomes a criminal if he has an "excess of definitions favorable to the violation of law," and because definitions are taken from significant others who, then, serve as reference categories or as reference groups for the person.

However, Sutherland's theory of differential association has had only limited success in explaining white collar criminality. There have been numerous criticisms leveled against Sutherland's "differential association theory," and the most obvious are:

1. The postulation of differential association does not provide a systematic theory or explain such crimes committed in the heat of passion or compulsive crimes.

2. He apparently had no clear conception of the learning process as his theory over simplifies it.

3. Finally, the structure of Sutherland's orientation was such as to make it difficult to test empirically (Caldwell, 1956:182-185) although resourceful attempts have been made to do this (De Fleur and Quinney, 1966:1-22).

In the 1950's Reckless and Dinitz have been attempting to discover how some lower-class families "insulate" their children against delinquency by virtue of the kind of parent-child relationships that were established. Although their empirical research model deals with juvenile delinquency rather than adult criminality, the Reckless model seems quite appropriate for criminal behavior.

Reckless states that:

> Insulation against delinquency on the part of these boys may be viewed as an on-going process reflecting an internalization of non-delinquent values and conformity to the expectations of significant others. . . . The research does not

indicate how the boy in the high delinquency area acquired
his self image. It may have been acquired by social definition of role from significant figures in his milieu such
as a mother, a relative, a priest, etc. . . . (1956:744-746)
(1957:566-590).

To be more explicit, Reckless generalized that a "good boy" self-conception had

a "negative" influence on delinquency and served as a deterrent to future crime.

The crucial variables Reckless uses in delinquency or non-delinquency

seems to be:

1. significant others; that is, the boy's internalization of these
    salient others becomes his self-image.

2. the presence of positive or negative reference groups as he
    refers to certain significant others as vital in the develop-
    ment of a "good boy" self-image or self-conception (1957:566).

Reckless concludes that certain concept(s) of self and of others con-

stitute the impact of life on the person as he internalizes his experience.

The self consists of the residues of attitudes and meanings accumulated through

the interaction (process) of an individual in interpersonal relations. Ap-

propriate or inappropriate concepts of self and others together comprise a model

of socio-psychological development and each may equally involve a normal de-

velopment (1957:570).

In the last decade, D. G. Glaser has reformulated and modified

Sutherland's "differential association theory" into a concept of differential

identification in order to emphasize that associations alone are not suf-

ficient to explain the adoption of criminality.

As Glaser further states:

    Most persons in our society are believed to identify them-
    selves with both criminal and noncriminal persons in the course
    of their lives. Criminal identification may occur, for example,

21

during direct experience in delinquent membership groups, through positive reference to criminal roles portrayed in mass media, or as a negative reaction to forces opposed to crime. The family probably is the principal noncriminal reference group, even for criminals. It is supplemented by many other anticriminal 'generalized others.'

The theory of differential identification in essence, is that a person pursues criminal behavior to the extent that he identifies himself with real or imaginary persons from whose perspective his criminal behavior seems acceptable. Such a theory focuses attention on the interaction in which choice of models occurs, including the individual's interaction with himself in rationalizing his conduct. This focus makes differential identification theory integrative; in that it provides a criterion of the relevance, for each individual case of criminality, of economic conditions, prior frustrations, learned moral creeds, group participation, or other features of an individual's life. These features are relevant to the extent that they can be shown to affect the choice of the other from whose perspective the individual views his own behavior (1956:440).

Glaser's theory of differential identification assumes that criminal behavior is the end product of identification with real or imaginary criminals. When the individual selects criminal models, he views his own behavior from their viewpoint and internalizes their codes, values, and attitudes. Thus, he is able to rationalize his behavior because criminal behavior seems acceptable. Differential identification theory seemingly offers a more fruitful approach since it not only attempts to account for social action but also for resultant interaction that takes place in the thought processes of man. Glaser does admit however that differential identification does not account for all crimes particularly accidental crimes, crimes of passion, or the lone crime.

Finally, Nardini, in his analysis of 128 first-time inmates at the Iowa State Penitentiary, attempted to verify the differential identification orientation (Reckless, 1967:399).

The criminological theory as developed from self-theory points to the lack of empirical testing. Sutherland's theory in particular demonstrated this void which Reiss and Rhodes attempt to fill through an empirical test (1964:5-18). Glaser's restatement of Sutherland's "differential association theory" directs it within a theoretical framework. Within the framework of differential identification this study focuses on the female criminal's self-conception as derived from the self-reference group theory. Application of the reference group theory variables to female offenders in a penal institution is clarified in the following discussion of the conceptual variables.

The Conceptual Processes

This research is a study of the female criminal's self-perception as related to criminality and to criminal self-conception. Analysis begins with the original self-conception. The individual is viewed as an object consisting of a series of attitudes. A self-conception is the refined attitude the inmate holds toward herself as a distinct social object (Kuhn, McPartland, 1954:68-75).

It is the assumption of this study that if a female prisoner does or does not think of herself as a criminal, it is because of those refined or organized attitudes toward self that are presumably reflected or derived from her reference groups as she perceives them.

In order to measure effects of reference groups, an operational definition is required. Newcomb apparently makes no differentiation between a reference group for self-identity and the reference to the individual by the group. There is no indication as to how the positive reference group "in which a person is motivated to be accepted" identifies or refers to the individual. According to Kuhn:

It (self) consists of the individual's attitudes
toward his own mind and body, viewed as an object.
. . . by referring to himself as a member of the groups
that he feels identify him, or to social categories which
his reference groups hold to be significant in identifying
him, or, finally, to evaluations of himself which hinge on
norms held by his reference groups. Whichever of these
referents he chooses, ... (Hickman, Kuhn, 1956:43-44).

This statement seems to indicate that the individual may refer to a group he feels identifies him; in other words, to a social group whose opinions he values, or to the category he perceives as the means by which this special group refers to him, or identifies him. Thus, it would appear that a reference group could be a positive or a negative reference, depending upon the group's reference to the individual.

The definition of the term "referent" should recognize two dimensions: (1) the significant others, or those whose opinions or judgments of her and her bahavior the inmate considers important, and (2) the regard of significant others, as she perceives or imagines it. If the inmate perceives that her significant others regard her as "a criminal" her referent is negative; and if not as "a criminal" her referent is positive, the criminal referent being absent. In operational terms, the presence or absence of negative referent indicates a criminal reference by significant others.

A description and analysis of the labelling process by which others "create" the criminal is found in the works of Becker (1963), Schur (1969), and Cressey and Ward (1969:608-612). As previously stated, this study assumes that the inmate's attitudes may be derived from the attitudes of her special reference group and then ordered in her own self-conception. If the inmate perceives that her significant others consider her a criminal, i.e., she has a criminal referent, she may agree or accept this attitude by thinking of

herself in the same manner.[2] Also, if she is assigned the label "criminal,"
an inmate may reject such attitudes derived from those of her significant
others (as she perceives their referents to her). Thus, if she perceives
her referent as criminal, she may accept the reference category assigned
to her if her referent is not criminal, she would be expected to reject
any reference category which labels her as criminal. To understand her
reference category and the process of effective labelling, one must consider
her self-definition (Hickman, Kuhn, 1956:208), (Thomas, Thomas, 1928:572)
as derived from her referent or the response she makes in self-conception.
Her referent may also be largely ignored if her self-evaluation is so ex-
aggerated that she begins to perceive her behavior as much more serious than
one would ordinarily expect.

It is assumed that a criminal or non-criminal self-conception may
also be functionally related to those social variables which describe
violations of criminal law:

1. the type of crime for which she is convicted;

2. guilt, trial plea;

3. the length of time served in prison.

A crime is legally defined as " . . . any act or omission prohibited
by law and punishable by the state in its own judicial proceedings" (Clark,
Marshall, 1952:1-16).

Early common law which evolved from centuries of custom and usage,
divided crimes into three major forms: treason, felony, and misdemeanor.
Although the American criminal code divides crimes into felonies, including
the felony of treason, and misdemeanors, this general division is not

uniformly employed among state codes (Hartung, 1966). This classification makes it difficult to distinguish between crimes by designations such as a "felony" and "misdemeanor."

For the purpose of this study crimes were arbitrarily divided by this investigator into "serious" (a sentence of more than two years) or "less serious" (a sentence of less than two years). Serious crimes against the person included murder, manslaughter, assault, robbery, narcotics, abortion and such crimes against property as burglary, theft, fraud or embezzlement while less serious crimes included prostitution, disorderly conduct, forgery or false checks and non-support.

Guilt is expressed or denied in the plea of guilty, not guilty, or no contest entered by the offender at her trial. Commitment results from being found guilty by a criminal court regardless of the trial plea.

Prison time is the total amount of time served in prison. This includes the length of sentence for the present commitment (obviously, only that portion served to the time of the study) and any previous time served in prison. Previous prison time depends on the number of previous commitments and the length of sentence served for each. The length of sentence is dependent on the crime for which the inmate is convicted and is determined accordingly by the court of law.

Finally, it is the general assumption of this study that the inmate's perception of guilt may be central to a criminal self-conception. Perception of guilt is to be differentiated from the trial plea of guilt. Perception of guilt is the inmate's attitude toward the criminal act for which she was convicted. Shibutani states that, "Guilt involves a judgment of oneself from

26

the standpoint of his reference group" (1961:261). The feelings of guilt that an inmate has about her own criminal act may be influenced by whether she thinks significant others regard her as a criminal.

The General Hypothesis

At the conceptual level: A criminal self-conception is related to the inmate's perception of her own guilt.

The dependent variable is the criminal self-conception; all other variables are independent and determined by the inmate's present situation. Within the theoretical orientation of differential identification, this study attempts an explanation why female inmates do or do not think of themselves as criminals.

The Major Conceptual Hypothesis

The criminal or non-criminal self-conception of female inmates in a penal community is functionally related to:

1. the self-reference theory variables: negative referents and reference category,

2. the criminal variables: type of crime and time in prison,

3. and, the inmate's perception of guilt.

The Specific Conceptual Hypotheses

Hypothesis One

Those inmates who conceive of themselves as criminals will have reference groups whom they think perceive of them as criminals.

Sub-Hypothesis. Women inmates are more likely to mention significant others who think of them as criminals than do male inmates.

Hypothesis Two

Those inmates who do not conceive of themselves as criminals will
perceive their reference category as non-criminal.

Hypothesis Three

Inmates with a criminal self-conception will have committed more
serious crimes than inmates who do not have a criminal self-conception.

Sub-Hypothesis. Those inmates who do not have criminal self-conceptions
but who have committed a serious crime will not have negative referents.

Hypothesis Four

Those inmates who commit serious crimes will have reference groups
who they think perceive of them as criminals.

Hypothesis Five

Those inmates who define their criminal acts as serious will perceive
themselves as criminal, while those inmates who define their acts as less
serious will not perceive themselves as criminal.

Hypothesis Six

Those inmates who at present have a criminal self-conception will
have had a criminal self-conception when they arrived in the penal institution, while those inmates who do not at present have a criminal self-conception
did not have a criminal self-conception on arrival.

In conclusion, the above hypotheses concerning the two types of independent variables, as developed conceptually, are formulated in support of the general hypothesis concerning criminal or non-criminal self-conception. The instrument used for obtaining data to empirically test the specific hypotheses continues in the same theoretical framework and is discussed in the following chapter.

Annotated Footnotes to Chapter II

[1]Robert G. Caldwell, Criminology (The Ronald Press, New York, second edition, 1965), fn. 200. The Client-Centered Theory, based upon the client-centered, but nondirected, relationship with the therapist, is the process in which the client "becomes aware" of his situation and his problems. See Carl Rodgers, Client-Centered Therapy: Its Current Practice, Implications, and Theory (Houghton, Mifflin Company, Boston, 1951). According to Caldwell, Rodgers' form of self-theory places attention upon the client and his psychology rather than on the group and the cultural environment of the symbolic interaction approach.

[2]The individual may agree or disagree with a reference group. The reference group may or may not assign a criminal label (reference category) to the individual and the individual may or may not accept a reference category or "label" assigned to her.

CHAPTER III

METHODOLOGY

Introduction

This research is intended to provide knowledge of criminal self-conception of the female offender in a penal setting and to explain the relationship between criminal self-conception and other social variables descriptive of criminality.

The instrument is an adaptation of Nardini's study (1958); it is one of the first utilized to study the female offender and her criminal self-conception. The instrument was pre-tested in the Women's Reformatory at Rockwell City, Iowa, on a sample of 29 inmates. This chapter describes the manner in which the instrument was assembled and how the study was executed.

Research Data

The data for this study of female offenders was obtained from 123 voluntary participants at the Wisconsin Home for Women located near the village of Taycheedah, Wisconsin. The institution's total population was 164; however, the six inmates in isolation during their admission period were not counted as available population.[1] Included in the total population are 25 juvenile inmates.[2] The available adult population is 133.

The Wisconsin Home for Women is a medium security institution that at the time of the study employed 58 female and five male guards, five social

31

workers and an educational staff of twenty. There is a seven-foot Cyclone, six-barb wire fence surrounding the institutional area. The ideal population of the institution is 114. The three dormitories--Harris, Neprud, and Addams Halls have a capacity of 65, 65, and 40 respectively; each room has one to four beds. Harris and Neprud Halls are medium security dormitories; Addams Hall has a maximum security section. Windows are blocked, and the doors kept locked. There is also a Superintendent's dwelling and a chapel on the grounds. Remedial through college level courses are offered; vocational and education courses in homemaking, health, and hygiene are also offered.

On August 7, 1964, the questionnaire (Appendix A) was administered to the voluntary population in five consecutive groups: one in Harris Hall, and two each in Neprud and Addams Hall. As the inmate population assembled for lunch in consecutive groups of approximately 40 each, an effort was made to test groups immediately preceding and following the noon meal. The institution allowed testing only during recreational hours. Since the girls were unwilling to give up this routine recreation, the recreation period was extended to allow for the tests which were not completed prior to the noon meal. The total testing period for the five groups was of short duration, only about two and one-half hours in length.

Although communication was kept at a minimum, no doubt some did occur. Inmates were told of the research project and volunteers were asked to assemble in the lounge of their respective living units. The researcher indicated that efforts to gain rapport had thus far resulted in excellent cooperation. He then read a prepared announcement to the various assembled groups stressing their opportunity in a study of female offenders. The announcement also stated that the questionnaire was designed to provide research with a better understanding of the inmates' views of the prison situation and of the outside world. They were reminded of the importance of answering all questions, as carefully and correctly as possible, to provide accurate information. Finally, it was re-emphasized since the survey was being conducted for research purposes to ultimately help other female offenders, the tests would be held confidential; the completed questionnaires would _not_ be seen by institution officials, and therefore constituted no threat to their present situation. Not one volunteer of those assembled refused after the researcher's announcement and subsequent request for their participation. In general, the volunteer population seemed cooperative, and interested in the research study.[3]

Of the 123 inmates participating in the study, fifteen were classified as juvenile delinquents. This sample (108) comprised 81 per cent of the 133 available adult population. Three questionnaires were incomplete and not included in the final analysis. However, these three (2.8%) cases lost from the study population did not constitute any known bias that would distort the analysis of data or the findings of the survey. The data in the final analysis is 79 per cent of the available adult population.

Design of the Instrument

Sound methodological procedures stress that data for research be obtained with all possible economy and efficiency. This is especially true where time and research personnel are limited by available funds. Probably the best definition of an effective study is that given by Hyman and Sheatsley: ". . . (An) effective study is one which obtains the maximum of relevant information for the minimum expenditure of time, money, personnel and resources" (1954:52).

In general, the instrument (Appendix A) designed for the purpose of measuring the criminal self-conception of the offender in a penal setting was constructed as concisely as possible. The questions of direct information were closed-ended, i.e., to be answered by checking _yes_ or _no_, or by a one word response. However, four sections were open-ended questions allowing for the respondent to initiate specific relevant factors. This technique eliminates the responses resulting from a set of formulated statements. The questionnaire was pre-tested and modified accordingly for the institution at Taycheedah.

Part 1A was designed to obtain statements from each respondent indicating her self-definitions. She was given the following directions:

> There are twenty numbered blanks on the page below. Please write twenty answers to the question "WHO AM I?" in these blanks. Just give twenty different answers to this question. Answer as if you were giving the answer to yourself--not to somebody else. Write your answers in the order that they occur to you. Don't worry about logic or "importance." Go along fairly fast; the time for this part of the questionnaire is limited.[4]

This test is called the Twenty Statements Test (T.S.T.). The use of the T.S.T. in a penal setting hardly expects the inmate to state that she is a criminal; however, a number of self-derogatory statements could be expected. It does permit the researcher to see the inmate as she sees herself. Since the T.S.T. was administered first, the inmate was given no clue as to what was expected of her but was allowed to freely express herself. The researcher anticipated an insight of the inmate's general self perception before proceeding to the directive portion of the instrument.

Part 1 constitutes information of the inmate's background and family, as well as two unrelated questions directed to her personal viewpoint. These are:

Do you think that you received a fair trial before you were convicted and sent to prison?

YES_____   NO_____

and immediately following

Would you say that you are guilty of the crime for which you were convicted?

YES_____   NO_____

Part 2 attempts to determine the inmate's definition of a criminal. It was derived from an open ended pre-test (Nardini, 1958:108) in which the inmates were asked to answer the question, "What is a criminal? Make some statements to complete the following sentence, A CRIMINAL IS . . . ." This was done for the purpose of orienting the questionnaire to the inmate's frame of reference. This section was closed in the second pre-test (Nardini, 1958:121). Sixteen statements taken from the open-ended pre-test were used to complete the question: "I would say that a criminal is . . . . yes or no." In the completed form of the instrument, seven of these sixteen statements were retained (Nardini, 1958:136-138). Four statements are consensual and three are non-consensual. Since each of the four consensual statements is specific evidence indicating a criminal violates the criminal law, they are considered the characteristics constituting the "societal" category of a criminal. The inmate, when describing a criminal, may be describing a criminal such as herself (Shibutani, 1961). A "yes" answer to all four consensual statements provides an index for identifying a criminal category (Nardini, 1958).

Part 3, an open-ended question to determine significant others states: "In the numbered blanks below, please list those groups or people whose opinions or judgments of you and your behavior you consider important. (Do not give proper names. Simply specify their relationship to you.)" Ten numbered blanks are provided for their answers.

Part 4, also an open-ended question seeks to identify those individuals and groups who think of her as a criminal and states: "In the numbered blanks below please list those groups or people who think of you as a criminal. (Do not give proper names. Simply specify their relationship or connection to you.)" Ten numbered blanks are provided for the answers.

The two open-ended tests were administered in their original form by H. A. Mulford (doctoral dissertation, 1953).

Part 5 determines those in the penal community who think of her as a criminal. A closed-ended checked question states: "Which of the following individuals would you say think of you as a criminal?" Matron guards, Matron supervisors, Other inmates, An inmate friend, Social Worker, Teachers." Space is provided for a "yes" or "no" response to each.

Part 6 parallels Part 5 to determine "Which of the following (family) individuals would you say think of you as a criminal? (In the event you do not have a brother, sister, spouse, etc., write NONE.)" The nine family members for a check "yes" or "no" response include both immediate and extended family.

Part 7 asks "Have you ever thought of yourself as a criminal?" and if yes, then attempts to establish at what time in her life she first thought of herself as a criminal. This is accomplished by a "yes" or "no" check response to a series of questions determining her first police record and concluding with the legal process in time order for the present conviction, from arrest through court procedure, to arrival in the institution.

Part 8 allows the inmate to compare herself with other convicted criminals. She is first asked if she knows of any person(s) on the outside who have committed as serious, or a more serious crime, but received less sentence. Finally, she is asked: "Do you now think of yourself as a criminal? and How did you plead at your trial?"

Part 9 provides for additional information concerning the inmate's background: education, marital status, and the entry date and length of sentence in the institution.

Part 10 asks the inmate to identify and check in the space provided the offense for which she is presently committed. Crimes ranged from murder and manslaughter to the less serious prostitution.

Part 11 is an anchorage type question asking the inmate to list (by initials) the individuals she considers to be her three best friends, and then list (by initials) her three best friends within the institution itself. The purpose of these two questions is to determine the extent or amount of anchorage within the institution.

Part 12 is a lie scale and included as a validity check on the over-all performance of the respondent. It is composed of six questions within the range of "normal" behavior to be answered by a check "yes" or "no" response.

Although certain questions may not appear to be specifically directed toward the hypotheses, they do contribute indirectly to the final evaluation of the study. As previously stated, Part 1A allows the inmate to present her-self as she perceives her situation, but she may or may not volunteer a criminal self-conception. Part 11 directed toward anchorage is included for the first time in this type of study and may need refinement following evaluation of

the findings. Parts 1, 8, 9, and 10 contain considerable statistical information which when checked by official data[5] constitutes validity for the
directive information. Part 8 appears to be satisfactory as a further validity
check using the lie scale.

Parts 3, 4, 5, and 6 combine to determine and confirm the crucial
variable, negative referent. This allows the inmate "her own head" so to
speak as she is directed from the general to the specific open-ended questions,
followed by closed-ended check "yes" or "no" response for cross tabulation.
Thus, in order to have a negative referent she must indicate the same significant person (by relationship) in Part 3 as one "whose opinions or judgments
of you and your behavior you consider important," and in Part 4 as one "who
thinks of you as a criminal," and also in Part 5 or 6 by a "yes" check to
the corresponding relationship. This procedure eliminates interpretation from
the researcher as to whom he believes should be significant others as negative
referents, also allowing for the possibility of anchorage within the institution.

In summation, this chapter contains discussion of procedures followed
in the development, pre-testing and administering of the questionnaire used
for this study. The variables were operationally defined, and the sample and
research conditions discussed. Certain background information including age,
race, education and type of crime will be considered in a later part of this
study.

Annotated Footnotes to Chapter III

[1]All inmates in the process of admission are held in isolation under medical observation for a ten-day period or longer if medical attention is needed.

[2]In a prior agreement with Mrs. Marcia Simpson, Superintendent, the girls transferred from Wisconsin School for Girls at Oregon, Wisconsin, were not to be included as they had not been sentenced by a criminal court. All inmates were given the opportunity to volunteer in order to eliminate any suspicion or noncooperation which could have resulted had they been informed that this research included only those over 18 years of age.

[3]The researcher was present for testing in all groups. In addition, a matron guard was present for supervision. Mrs. Rudolph Bott, social work supervisor, notified the inmates of the research project and was also present in the testing situation.

[4]This section of the instrument was developed by Manford H. Kuhn and Thomas McPartland. See Manford H. Kuhn, "A Proposal for Classification of Self Theory," an unpublished manuscript, 1952. See also Thomas McPartland, "The Self and Social Structure: An Empirical Approach," an unpublished doctoral dissertation, State University of Iowa, 1953. Note as well "An Empirical Investigation of Self Attitudes," American Sociological Review, Volume 19, No. 1, February, 1954, pp. 68-72.

[5]Wisconsin Statutes Annotated, 1958, Volume 41, Section 939.01-947.15.

CHAPTER IV

FINDINGS

Introduction

The emphasis of this chapter is the statistical analysis of the data described in the preceding chapter and the statistical testing of the hypotheses stated in Chapter II concerning the criminal self-conception of female inmates. This analysis includes an interpretation of the findings within the theoretical framework of the study.

The findings presented are applicable only to those groups tested at the Wisconsin Home for Women at Taycheedah since there was not an opportunity for the selection of a random sample. Volunteer respondents are considered legitimate, as long as the shortcomings are realized between the data and the universe. In Chapter III the similarities between the inmates measured and the general characteristics of the total inmate population were noted. An attempt to secure data from the entire prison population at the Wisconsin Home for Women at Taycheedah was made, but this attempt fell short of covering the total prison population. However, data were obtained from 79 per cent (105 of 133 inmates). This incomplete data are "samples" only in the loosest sense of the term. The investigator is aware of the limitations of such incomplete data.

Statistical Procedure

Although no random sample is present, a test of significance will still be employed for their heuristic value. As many modern authorities suggest, in the absence of other criteria, the test of significance can almost always be useful in interpreting findings (Blalock 1960:270). As Winch and Campbell (1969:140) point out:

> . . . it is our judgment that although the test of significance is irrelevant to the interpretation of the cause of a difference, still it does provide a relevant and useful way of assessing the relative likelihood that a real difference exists and is worthy of interpretive attention, as opposed to the hypothesis that the set of data could be a haphazard arrangement.

The use of a significance test allows the investigator to eliminate chance as the "cause" of the observed relationship. Chi square is being used to test for this where applicable. In addition, phi squared is being used to measure the strength or degree of relationship present. This will permit comparisons to be made between the tables.

In the analyses, significant tests are assigned a minor role; instead stress is placed on the measure of associations, their strength, direction, and proportion of variation that is explained.

In this study involving two or more independent variables, the dependent variable is analyzed not only by the degree of association with the independent variable(s), but also by the degree of association. The data have been collected and checked against IBM institutional records for reliability, then analyzed for the hypothesized relationships.

Hypothesis One

<u>Those inmates who conceive of themselves as criminals will have</u>
<u>reference groups whom they think perceive them as criminals.</u>

The rationale for this hypothesis stems from the theoretical model
that the inmate, as any individual, is included to refer to those whose
opinions and judgments of her she considers important for self-identification.
If she thinks these significant others consider her to be a criminal, their
attitude may be reflected in her self-conception. The effect of this negative
referent on the inmate's self-perception is observed directly in her self-
conception. Negative referents are individually determined as they are
identified and indirectly confirmed by the respective inmate in her responses
to a series of specific items within several parts of the questionnaire. (see
Chapter III, page 38): The criminal self-conception is measured by asking
the inmate the direct closed-ended question: "Do you now think of yourself
as a criminal?" The procedure which establishes a criminal or non-criminal
self-conception has been described in Chapter III, page 37). (Part 8, question
number four). The T.S.T., however, was not analyzed for criminal self-conception due to inmate failure to complete twenty statements.

In Table 1 the inmate's self-conception (criminal or non-criminal) is
presented in the rows and negative reference groups (present or absent) are
shown in the columns.

In Table 1, 62 per cent of the female inmates with a criminal self-
conception have negative referents present; 38 per cent do not. The relationship is in the direction predicted by hypothesis one. Although not specifically predicted, it is interesting to observe three-fourths of those females

TABLE 1

CRIMINAL SELF-CONCEPTION AND NEGATIVE REFERENTS

Self-Conception	NEGATIVE REFERENTS				
	Present		Absent		
	N	(%)	N	(%)	Total
Criminal	21	(62)	13	(38)	34
Non-Criminal	18	(25)	53	(75)	71
TOTAL	39		66		105

ϕ^2 = .13, x^2 = 13.56, p < .001

with a non-criminal self-conception have negative referents absent. A chi square of 13.56 is significant at the .001 level. It is highly unlikely that this relationship occurred by chance because the ϕ^2 has been computed to measure the strength of relationship. The ϕ^2 is .13 and shows that about 13 per cent of the variation in criminal self-conception is explained by the presence or absence of negative referents.

The data presented supports the hypothesis that inmates who have reference groups whom they think perceive them as criminals think of themselves as criminals. Also, those inmates who do not think of themselves as criminals are less likely to have referents who think of them as criminal.

Sub-Hypothesis One

Women inmates will more likely mention significant others who think of them as criminals than do male inmates.

43

According to criminologists, the rationale of this hypothesis is that women in our society tend to be more protected and shielded from being reported, arrested, tried, and convicted of criminal offenses than men. This is no doubt due to the differential treatment and action of the court system. Once she is finally convicted, however, society tends to be more severe in its condemnation of her.

In order to test this hypothesis, data from the Nardini study (doctoral dissertation, 1958) (see Table 23, Appendix B) was incorporated in Table 2 containing the presence or absence of negative referents groups of male inmates and compared with data from female inmates of this study.

Table 2 reveals the relationship between males and females in the columns, with the presence or absence of negative referents in the rows.

TABLE 2

NEGATIVE REFERENTS AND SEX OF INMATE

Negative Referents	Male		Female		Total
	N	(%)	N	(%)	
Present	80	(63)	39	(37)	119
Absent	48	(37)	66	(63)	114
TOTAL	128		105		233

$\phi^2 = .14$, $x^2 = 34.18$, $p < .001$

In Table 2, the association is in the unexpected direction. The sub-hypotheses, as originally formulated, states female inmates are more likely to identify significant others who think of them as criminal than do male inmates. In the observed relationship, however, more male inmates identify negative referents than female inmates, and a x^2 of 34.18 is statistically significant at the .001 level. A ϕ^2 of .14 explains fourteen per cent of the variation observed in Table 2. This data strongly disconfirms the hypothesis as stated.

In summation, the investigator is aware of the limitations of comparing these two sets of data since the number of previous offenses could not be controlled in the data on female inmates. It is noted, male inmates who are incarcerated for the first time, report negative referents more than females. This could be the result of either negative referents not occurring or less impact on female inmates who are no longer sensitive to negative referents because of previous experiences in prison.

Hypothesis Two

Those inmates who do not conceive of themselves as criminals will perceive their reference category as non-criminal.

The rationale for this hypothesis is a continuation of hypothesis one with emphasis on a non-criminal self-conception. According to self theorists, the individual (or inmate) defines herself in terms that her significant others use to define or refer to her appropriate behavior (Hickman, Kuhn, 1956:43-44). As the result of being placed in a category by significant others, the inmate will refer to the same category to identify herself. It should be recalled that the category is operationalized as previously defined by societal group, specifically inmate group. The inmate's reference category is the category by which her significant others refer to her; in other words the individual's reference category is the category of her referents.

45

The inmates who do not describe a criminal by the accepted classification definition may be directly reflecting the absence of criminal referents by not thinking of themselves as criminal. The presence or absence of criminal category can be viewed as her corresponding referents category. If the inmates who do not describe the category as criminal do not have criminal referents, the non-criminal category is their reference category as perceived in the absence of criminal referents.

A criminal index was constructed from the results of Part (2) of the questionnaire where the inmate is asked to indicate whether she personally would or would not make certain statements about a criminal. Seven statements were made with an opportunity for the inmate to indicate agreement or disagreement. An assumption is made that the inmate must answer "yes" to the first four statements and "no" to the last three statements in order to identify a criminal in the same manner as society would. On the basis of these responses inmates were classified as being in either a criminal or a non-criminal category as further substantiation of a crude index of criminality for each inmate. A further assumption is made that the inmate's responses indicate her "true" criminal referents category. In other words, the inmate is reflecting her perception of criminal or non-criminal referents. It is her perception of the terms that her referents use towards her. This assumption is based upon Kuhn's interpretation of referents (1956:43-44).

The criminal self-conception is determined by the inmates response "Do you now think of yourself as a criminal?" Those answering in the affirmative are classified as having a criminal self-conception; whereas, those answering negatively to the above question are classified as having a non-criminal self-conception.

46

TABLE 3

SELF-CONCEPTION AND INDEX OF CRIMINAL CATEGORY

Self-Conception	CRIMINAL CATEGORY				
	Present		Absent		
	N	(%)	N	(%)	Total
Criminal	17	(50)	17	(50)	34
Non-Criminal	22	(31)	48	(69)	70
TOTAL	39		65		104

ϕ^2 = .03, x^2 = 2.97, .10 > p > .05

In Table 3 the columns represent the inmate's criminal category, index presence or absence, and the rows represent the inmate's reported self-conception, criminal or non-criminal. The findings in Table 3 indicate the relationship is not significant at the .05 level. A ϕ^2 of .03 that the independent variable explains about three per cent of the variation observed in Table 3.

In summation, although the data are not statistically significant, the direction of the relationship with respect to non-criminal self-conception and criminal referent categories, lends tentative support to the hypothesis.

Hypothesis Three

Inmates with a criminal self-conception will have committed more serious crimes than inmates who do not have a criminal self-conception.

It is reasonable to assume the inmates who perceive themselves as criminals have committed a serious crime. Committing a serious crime is judged to be a relevant factor in the development of criminal self-conception, directly or indirectly, through the inmates' significant other referents. As previously defined, serious crimes are criminal offenses against the person and felonies against property; less serious crimes are misdemeanor offenses and sex offenses. (See Chapter II, page 26 for operational definition of type of crime.) The criminal self-conception is determined by the inmates answer to: "Do you now think of yourself as a criminal?"

Table 4 presents the type of crime for this commitment (serious or less serious) in the columns, and female inmates' self-conception in the rows.

TABLE 4

FEMALE INMATES' SELF-CONCEPTION AND TYPE OF CRIME

	TYPE OF CRIME				
	Serious		Less Serious		
Self-Conception	N	(%)	N	(%)	Total
Criminal	24	(71)	10	(29)	34
Non-Criminal	34	(48)	37	(52)	71
TOTAL	58		47		105

$\phi^2 = .04$, $x^2 = 4.41$, $.05 > p > .02$

The data in Table 4 indicates an association between type of crime and self-conception. Seventy-one per cent of the inmates who had committed a serious crime have a criminal self-conception while 29 per cent of those who had committed a less serious crime have a criminal self-conception. This relationship is significant at the .05 level and would eliminate the explanation due to chance.

Phi-squared of .04 would indicate that only four per cent of the variation in criminal self-conception is explained by its association with type of crime. Although type of crime is apparently a factor, this shows it is less important in producing a criminal self-conception than the presence or absence of negative referents discussed earlier.

In summary, this finding supports the hypothesis that inmates who hold a criminal self-conception are more likely to have committed a serious crime. The results examined in this study, however, suggest that the magnitude of serious criminal behavior alone may not be sufficient to produce a criminal self-conception. Consideration of this point is the concern of sub-hypothesis.

Sub-Hypothesis Three

Those inmates who do not have a criminal self-conception but who have committed a serious crime will not have negative referents.

In Table 4 it is noted that 52 per cent (37) of the inmates who do not have a criminal self-conception had committed a less serious crime compared to 48 per cent (34) who had committed a serious crime. Sub-hypothesis three considers the relationship between negative referents and self-conception while controlling for serious crime.

TABLE 5

THE RELATIONSHIP BETWEEN SELF-CONCEPTION AND
NEGATIVE REFERENTS CONTROLLING FOR SERIOUS CRIME

	SERIOUS CRIMES NEGATIVE REFERENTS				
	Present		Absent		
Self-Conception	N	(%)	N	(%)	Total
Criminal	16	(67)	8	(33)	24
Non-Criminal	10	(29)	24	(71)	34
TOTAL	26		32		58

$\phi^2 = .12$, $x^2 = 7.18$, $.01 > p > .001$

In Table 5, 71 per cent (24 of 34) of the inmates who had committed a serious crime do not report negative referents; nor do they report a criminal self-conception. A chi-square of 7.14 is statistically significant beyond the .01 level. It is highly unusual that the relationship occurred by chance. The computed phi-squared is .12. Twelve per cent of the variation observed is explained by the independent variable negative referents. Inmates who do not have a criminal self-conception but have committed a serious crime are more likely to report negative referents absent. Thus, sub-hypothesis three is supported as stated.

TABLE 6

THE RELATIONSHIP BETWEEN SELF-CONCEPTION AND
TYPE OF CRIME CONTROLLING FOR NEGATIVE REFERENTS

	PARTIAL A. Negative Referents Present Type of Crime					PARTIAL B. Negative Referents Absent Type of Crime				
	Serious		Less Serious			Serious		Less Serious		
Self-Conception	N	(%)	N	(%)	Total	N	(%)	N	(%)	Total
Criminal	16	(62)	5	(38)	21	8	(25)	5	(15)	13
Non-Criminal	10	(38)	8	(62)	18	24	(75)	29	(85)	53
TOTAL	26		13		39	32		34		66

Partial A. $\phi^2 = .05$, $x^2 = 1.86$, $.20 > p > .10$

Partial B. $\phi^2 = .01$, $x^2 = .86$, $.50 > p > .30$

The total relationship of Table 4 and Table 6 illustrates a situation in which the control variable, criminal referents, is relevant to a statistically significant relationship because the association found in Table 4 between type of crime and self-conception virtually disappears when absence of criminal referents is held constant. The investigation concludes the presence or absence of negative referents explains the relationship between type of crime and non-criminal self-conception. This becomes obvious when examining the column totals in Partial A and B, Table 6: 80 per cent (53) of the 66 inmates who state they have no negative referents do not perceive of themselves as criminal. In contrast, 54 per cent (21) of the 39 inmates who have negative referents reveal they think themselves criminals.

In summation, it is evident from the findings, inmates who have a criminal self-conception will have committed a serious crime; however, the negative referents factor seems to be the more crucial link between type of crime and inmate's reporting a non-criminal conception.

Hypothesis Four

Those inmates who commit serious crimes will have reference groups who they think perceive of them as criminals.

The rationale for the above is, committing a serious crime should evoke perception of criminal referents by the inmate more than the one who commits a less serious crime. The concern of this hypothesis is the relation-ship of crime to criminal reference. The question raised is: Is seriousness of crime directly related to criminal reference or indirectly related through the inmate's perception which is reflected in the identity of her self-conception?

In order to test the relationship between crime and negative reference the relevant data are presented in Table 7. Type of crime was determined from the inmate's response to the offense for which she is pre-sently committed and then confirmed with institutional data, and then this crime was classified as serious or less serious.

TABLE 7

THE RELATIONSHIP BETWEEN NEGATIVE REFERENCE AND TYPE OF CRIME

| | NEGATIVE REFERENCE | | | | |
| | Present | | Absent | | |
Type of Crime	N	(%)	N	(%)	Total
Serious	26	(45)	32	(55)	58
Less Serious	13	(28)	34	(72)	47
TOTAL	39		66		105

ϕ^2 = .03, x^2 = 3.34, .10 > p > .05

There is no statistically significant relationship between the two independent variables. A x^2 of 3.34 and a ϕ^2 of .03 which accounts for only three per cent of the variation observed in the relationship. Only 45 per cent of those inmates who have committed a serious crime report negative referents. Statistically, the data fail to support the hypothesis as formulated. As the rationale suggested, inmates who have committed serious crimes would be more likely to promote and view referents from groups who think of them as criminals. It is possible to pursue the analysis of apparently non-significant results in order to uncover salient factors which would indicate that, while the original relationship is not significant, specification would indicate a relationship of negative reference which is not related to present crime but does emerge from earlier crimes and convictions. Of the 105 inmates in the original data, information on prior commitments was not available for 13. Where such information was available, 85 (92 per cent) had prior periods of incarcertaion (Table 21, Appendix B). This information implies that prior felony or a serious crime may suggest negative (criminal) reference. A crude time order may be attained when controlling for two or more previous felonies. According to David Abrahamsen (1960:126), when an inmate has committed a crime for the third time, he is designated a chronic offender. The cutting point of two or more or one or less felonies was decided mainly on two criteria: (1) nearly all inmates had previous felonies prior to their present conviction; 58 inmates had had two or more commitments and 34 had only one prior conviction; (2) a person who cimmits three crimes would be designated a chronic offender. This classification also rests upon the seriousness of the criminal act which in turn reflects the amount of the criminal's personality involvement.

Table 8 indicates female inmates who have had prior periods of incarceration due to previous felonies and the type of crime for the present commitment. Information for the type of crime resulting in present incarceration was confirmed with institutional records as well as for previous incarceration(s).

A ϕ^2 of .05, a x^2 of 4.74 indicates a statistically significant association at the .05 level, and a percentage differential of 25 is observed. It is thus not likely that the observed relationship occurred by chance. Table 8 suggests that more than one felony or a series of crimes is associated with the inmates' type of crime (serious or less serious) and present commitment. Of the 58 inmates with two or more prior felony commitments, 38 or 66 per cent have committed a serious crime for this incarceration.

TABLE 8

THE RELATIONSHIP BETWEEN FEMALE INMATES WITH PRIOR
FELONY COMMITMENTS AND TYPE OF CRIME

| | PRIOR FELONIES | | | | |
| | Two or More | | One or Less | | |
Type of Crime	N	(%)	N	(%)	Total
Serious	38	(66)	14	(41)	52
Less Serious	20	(34)	20	(59)	40
TOTAL	58		34		92

$\phi^2 = .05$, $x^2 = 4.74$, $.05 > p > .02$

Among the 34 inmates with one or less prior felony commitments 14, or 41 per cent, are committed for a serious crime.

As was observed in Table 7, negative referents were not found to be strongly related to present crime. Would the relationship intensify if earlier crimes and commitments were introduced as a control variable?

In testing a "crude" time order, the relationship between present commitment and negative referents controlling for two or more serious crimes is considered in Table 9.

TABLE 9

THE RELATIONSHIP BETWEEN PRESENT COMMITMENT AND
NEGATIVE REFERENTS CONTROLLING FOR TWO OR MORE PRIOR FELONIES

	PARTIAL A. Two or More Previous Felonies					PARTIAL B. One or Less Previous Felonies				
Negative Reference	Serious		Less Serious			Serious		Less Serious		
	N	(%)	N	(%)	Total	N	(%)	N	(%)	Total
Present	17	(45)	3	(15)	20	6	(43)	9	(45)	15
Absent	21	(55)	17	(85)	38	8	(57)	11	(55)	19
TOTAL	38		20		58	14		20		34

Table 9, Partial A, reveals a percentage differential of 30.

Those inmates who have committed two or more felonies and have com-mitted a serious crime for their present commitment (17 or 45 per cent) are more likely to have had negative referents than inmates who commit a less serious crime for this current commitment (3 or 15 per cent).

Partial B reveals a percentage differential of 2. This partial as-sociation (Table 9) specifies the original Table 8 and suggests the relation-ship holds for only inmates with two or more previous felony commitments. Thus, the degree and direction of the relationship has been specified by previous felonies. It would appear, criminal factors (previous felonies and commitments) merge with present type of crime; therefore, it is not possible to analyze the relationship of previous commitments to criminal referents and self-conception. In other words, it is not possible to prorate criminal referents to crime since it is cumulative from criminal experience.

In summation, hypothesis four was not substantiated. Hypothesis four would have to be reformulated to take into account previous criminal felonies. Because of the ex post facto nature of this study, coupled with the presence of previous penal experience, there are no data to measure when negative referents occurred prior to the inmate's present crime and incarceration.

Hypothesis Five

Those inmates who define their criminal acts as serious will perceive themselves as criminal, while those inmates who define their acts as less serious will not perceive themselves as criminal.

The rationale stems from W. I. Thomas: "If men define situations as real they are real in their consequences" (1923).

Each inmate is responsible for her situation: that is, she has been convicted and incarcerated for violation of a criminal law. But the concern of the hypothesis was the inmate's definition of the seriousness of her crime as it relates to her concept of self.

For the inmate to achieve a certain degree of clarity in self-definition involves an evaluation of her criminal behavior. This process is simply the conspective act during which the inmate reviews her past and evaluates her present situation with the aim of self-assessment, self-indication, and which terminates in a particular self-conception.

Symbolic-interactionist theory provides a framework which deals with the relationship between the inmates' behavior and self-identification. The inmate looks upon herself as an _object_, identifying herself as a particular kind of person; for example, as a criminal.

In our present situation one cannot be entirely sure how the inmate arrives at a particular identity. According to Ehrlich, "The exact behavior that complements a specific attitude is not always clear, and the presumed clarity of an act is itself a consequence of the perspective from which it is evaluated as well as the time that intervenes between the act and evaluation" (1969:33). When engaging in a self-analysis, the inmate may focus on another inmate and draw a comparison in order to determine her own self-conception. If knowledge of others who commit more serious crimes is present, this process may allow the inmate to evaluate her own act as serious (or less serious) and thus to form her concept of self. Almost every criminal attempts to gain this kind of perspective by viewing her crime in comparison to what others have done.

In order to determine how the inmate views or perceives her own crime, a series of methodological steps are employed. First, she must identify the criminal category. If she does, the investigator is aware that she can (or does) recognize the norms of society. If she does not identify the criminal category, the investigator does not know how the inmate identifies a criminal. That is, she may have any number of ways by which she identifies a criminal category.[1] Second, those inamtes who identify a criminal category are compared to the investigator's classification (type of crime) using the inmate's present commitment.

In other words, if the inmate tends to agree that she has committed a serious crime, she is likely to have a criminal self-conception. If she does not concur, she will be more apt to have a non-criminal self-conception. Finally, the inmate is compared to a "crude" index, using her knowledge of many who have committed more serious crimes (with reference to the researcher's classification of type of crime). If she has committed a serious crime and defines her crime as a serious one, this definition should result in a criminal self-conception. If she knows of many who have committed more serious crimes but defines her crime as less serious, she will tend to have a non-criminal self-conception.

TABLE 10

CRIMINAL SELF-CONCEPTION AND CRIMINAL CATEGORY

| | CRIMINAL CATEGORY | | | |
Self-Conception	Present N (%)	Absent N (%)	Total
Criminal	30 (88)	4 (12)	34
Non-Criminal	37 (52)	34 (48)	71
TOTAL	67	38	105

$\phi^2 = .11$, $x_y^2 = 11.47$, $p < .001$

Table 10 was computed using Yates' correction (Walker, Lev, 1953:106).

Table 10 shows a relationship that is statistically significant at the .001 level, which would eliminate chance occurrence. A x^2 of 13.56 and a phi-squared of .11. A percentage difference of 36 is noted. The above finding indicates an association between a criminal self-conception and identification of the criminal category.

The function of the Table, however, is to reveal those (67) inmates who were able to identify the criminal category in a comparative manner to normative society.

The second operation is concerned with those inmates who did identify the criminal category, which is held constant, and the inmate's self-conception is tested against the type of crime for her present commitment.

TABLE 11

THE RELATIONSHIP BETWEEN TYPE OF CRIME
AND SELF-CONCEPTION CONTROLLING FOR CRIMINAL CATEGORY

	CRIMINAL CATEGORY IDENTIFIED BY INMATES				
	Type of Crime				
	Serious		Less Serious		
Self-Conception	N	(%)	N	(%)	Total
Criminal	23	(77)	7	(23)	30
Non-Criminal	17	(46)	20	(54)	37
TOTAL	40		27		67

ϕ^2 = .10, x^2 = 6.28, .02 > p > .01

Table 11 shows a ϕ^2 of .10 and a x^2 of 6.28 which is statistically significant at the .02 level. A percentage difference of 31 is also noted. Of those inmates who have identified a criminal category, 77 per cent, or 23 inmates, have a criminal self-conception and have committed serious crimes while 54 per cent, or 20 inmates, do not have a criminal self-conception but have committed less serious crimes. As can readily be seen in Table 11, the relationship between type of crime and self-conception is observed when controlling for identification of criminal category.

The inmate's definition of a serious crime was determined by her identification of a criminal category and measured by her response to the following statement, "Would you say that there are many people who have committed a more serious crime than you have . . .?" The "yes" or "no" response to the above statement was measured against the criminal self-conception and the inmate's crime for her present commitment.

TABLE 12

AWARENESS OF OTHERS COMMITTING SERIOUS CRIMES

	PARTIAL A. YES Criminal Category Type of Crime					PARTIAL B. NO Criminal Category Type of Crime				
	Serious		Less Serious			Serious		Less Serious		
Self-Conception	N	(%)	N	(%)	Total	N	(%)	N	(%)	TOTAL
Criminal	20	(77)	6	(23)	26	3		1		4
Non-Criminal	14	(48)	15	(52)	29	3		5		8
TOTAL	34		21		55	6		6		12

Partial A. $\phi^2 = .09$, $x^2 = 4.94$, $.05 > p > .02$

Partial B. (For Descriptive Purpose Only)

Table 12, Partial A, shows a statistical relationship with a x^2 of 4.94 that is significant at the .05 level and a ϕ^2 of .09. The findings indicate that 77 per cent or 20 inmates, who have committed serious crimes do have a criminal self-conception and define their crime as serious. Also, the findings show that 52 per cent, or 15 inmates, who have committed less serious crimes do not have a criminal self-conception and define their crimes as less serious. Partial B is presented for descriptive purpose only as the cell frequencies are insufficient for meaningful statistical interpretation

In summation, hypothesis five has been supported as stated by the above statistical association. In general, this process of self-identity may force on the inmate a harsh comparison with others who have committed more serious crimes and in the final phase the development of more mature criminal self-conception.

Hypothesis Six

Those inmates who at present have a criminal self-conception will have had a criminal self-conception when they arrived in the penal institution, while those inmates who do not at present have a criminal self-conception did not have a criminal self-conception on arrival.

The consistency of a self-conception is the concern of this hypothesis. The rationale in general implies that stability of self is apparently necessary in order to operate meaningfully in any situation, but if situations develop to alter its effectiveness (of the self), a redefining of self may eventually occur. Recognizing the apparent similarity of attitudes in the inmate's self-conception and those of her significant others but considering the necessity of a responsible consistency in self-conception, an ill-defined or an unstable situation may produce an alteration of self.

This study is also concerned with the influence of incarceration on the self-conception, i.e., does the inmate's self-conception remain relatively stable in spite of demands placed on her by institutionalization? What effect, if any, does prisonization have on the self-conception?

It is to be remembered that on arrival in prison the inmate has just passed through a "stripping process" where the outside world values are possibly no longer appropriate for maintaining her former self-conception. The offender's recent court experience may have created a psychological impression that could be called a "state of shock." Also the inmate's inter-personal network has been disrupted and perception of disapproval from her significant others may bring forth "self-condemnation" which could ultimately lead to redefinition. If the inmate continues to correspond to significant others whom whe still favors for support, then knowledge or belief that they may think of her negatively after her conviction may result from feel-ings of guilt. Consequently, if at any time an inmate were to think of her-self as a criminal, arrival in the penal institution would seemingly be the most reasonable time. During adjustment to the prison community, the inmate's self-conception probably stabilizes.

The inmate is evaluated with respect to self-conception both at the time of admission and at the time of the study.

Table 13 is statistically significant at the .001 level, with a x^2 of 14.56 and a ϕ^2 of .14. A percentage difference of .35 is substantial. The results are clear cut that females who had a criminal self-conception upon

TABLE 13

THE RELATIONSHIP BETWEEN CRIMINAL SELF-CONCEPTION
UPON ARRIVAL (IN THE WISCONSIN HOME FOR WOMEN) AND
THE INMATES SELF-CONCEPTION AT THE TIME OF STUDY

| | SELF-CONCEPTION ON ARRIVAL | | | | |
Self-Conception	Criminal N	(%)	Non-Criminal N	(%)	Total
Criminal	29	(47)	5	(12)	34
Non-Criminal	33	(53)	38	(88)	71
TOTAL	62		43		105

$\phi^2 = .14$, $x^2 = 14.56$, $p < .001$

arrival continued to perceive themselves as criminal when measured in the penal institution. That is, 47 per cent (29 inmates) had a criminal self-conception upon arrival and at the time of the study; whereas 12 per cent (5 inmates) who now have a criminal self-conception did not perceive of themselves as criminal upon admission. As can be seen, 41 per cent (43 inmates) who did not have a criminal self-conception at the time of admission and, at present, 88 percent (or 38 inmates) still did not visualize themselves as criminal.

In summation, then, Table 13 supports hypothesis six. Those women who view themselves now as criminals also tended to have a criminal self-conception on commitment, and those who did not view themselves as criminal on commitment still tend to view themselves as non-criminal.

In addition it was felt that an opportunity existed to test for
serious crimes at the time of arrival which may help interpret the effect
of the seriousness of the inmates criminal act upon the inmates self-conception.

TABLE 14

THE RELATIONSHIP BETWEEN CRIMINAL SELF-CONCEPTION UPON ARRIVAL
IN THE PENAL INSTITUTION AND CRIMINAL SELF-CONCEPTION AT
THE TIME OF THE STUDY CONTROLLING FOR TYPE OF CRIME

	PARTIAL A.				PARTIAL B.			
	Serious Crime on Arrival				Less Serious Crime on Arrival			
	Criminal		Non-Criminal			Criminal		Non-Criminal		
Self-Conception	N	(%)	N	(%)	Total	N	(%)	N	(%)	Total
Criminal	21	(55)	3	(15)	24	8	(33)	2	(9)	10
Non-Criminal	17	(45)	17	(85)	34	16	(67)	21	(91)	37
TOTAL	38		20		58	24		23		47

In Table 14, Partial A, 66 per cent (38) of those inmates who had committed a serious crime for this offense had a criminal self-conception upon
arrival, and 55 per cent (21) still had a criminal self-conception at the time
of the study.

In comparison as shown in Partial B, 49 per cent (23) of all those
inmates who had committed a less serious crime did not have a criminal self-
conception upon arrival in the penal institution, and 91 per cent (21) still
did not have a criminal self-conception at the time of the study.

The data indicates that the inmate who on arrival had committed a serious crime would be more apt to have a criminal self-conception than if she had committed a less serious crime; however, at the time of the study only 55 per cent (21) of those inmates who had committed a serious crime would still have such a criminal self-conception at the time of the study compared to 91 per cent (21) of those inmates who had committed less serious crimes who did not have it on arrival and still would not have a criminal self-conception at the time when measured.

Since it was apparent earlier (see hypothesis four) that inmates had previous felonies prior to the present commitment an interesting relationship would show the effects of previous incarcerations on self-conception.

TABLE 15

THE RELATIONSHIP BETWEEN CRIMINAL SELF-CONCEPTION UPON
ARRIVAL IN THE PENAL INSTITUTION AND CRIMINAL
SELF-CONCEPTION AT THE TIME OF THE STUDY
CONTROLLING FOR PREVIOUS FELONIES

| | PARTIAL A. Two or More Previous Felonies | | | | | PARTIAL B. One or Less Previous Felony | | | | |
| | Criminal | | Non-Criminal | | | Criminal | | Non-Criminal | | |
Self-Conception	N	(%)	N	(%)	Total	N	(%)	N	(%)	Total
Criminal	21	(58)	3	(14)	24	4	(14)	1	(6)	5
Non-Criminal	15	(42)	19	(86)	34	14	(86)	15	(94)	29
TOTAL	36		22		58	18		16		34

The reader should remember that 92 inmates had had prior felonies and

66

incarcerations before their present commitment.

In Table 15 of those inmates who had two or more previous felonies, 58 per cent (21) had a criminal self-conception upon arrival and still had it at the time studied while 86 per cent (19) who did not have a criminal self-conception upon arrival still did not perceive themselves criminal when tested for a criminal self-conception. As can be seen, Partial A is statistically significant and contributes meaningfully to the original relationship in Table 13. Partial B, on the other hand, shows no significant relationship. The inmate's self-conception as criminal may well be affected by their incarceration experiences.

In conclusion, the above findings relative to hypothesis six, indicate that inmates who have a criminal self-conception when studied, will in all probability have had it upon arrival in the penal institution. Also, if the inmate does not have a criminal self-conception at the time of the study she probably did not have a criminal self-conception upon arrival.

In this chapter, the testing and analysis of the hypotheses were presented and discussed. The findings demonstrated that the self-conception of female inmates is associative with significant others, criminal category, prior felonies, and definition of criminal acts as serious.

Annotated Footnote to Chapter IV

[1]In order to operationalize the data in Table 10, an assumption is made that the inmate recognizes what a criminal is by answering "yes" to questions 1, 2, 3 and 4 in Part 2 of the questionnaire. By answering all four questions "yes" she has a criminal category present. A further assumption is made that she does define a criminal with these statements, she could make these statements about herself.

CHAPTER V

SUMMARY AND CONCLUSION

The purpose of this dissertation was to study a central component
of the self, specifically the identification of a criminal self-conception
and the perception of self, as held by female inmates in a penal institution.
This research purports to be one of the first designed to study the female
inmate and her self-conception. Female inmates are a long neglected criminal
population and this study attempts to fill part of that void.

The theoretical orientation model of self-reference group theory
as formulated by Sutherland and later reformulated by Glaser guided the
hypotheses. The focus of this theory was upon the specific negative reference
groups which might simultaneously affect an inmate's criminal self-conception.
It was hypothesized that a criminal self-conception is functionally related
to the inmate's criminal acts, reference groups, reference categories, and
her definition of the situation. Many aspects of self-theory were not tested
in this study.

In Wisconsin, all adult female offenders who are sentenced to a
penal institution are remanded to the Wisconsin Home for Women at Taycheedah.
The data included seventy-nine per cent (105 of 133) of available inmates
in the penal institution on the day the questionnaire was administered.

Inmates who had insufficient education (Language comprehension and/or intelligence) to complete a pencil and paper questionnaire, as well as those inmates under 18 years of age, were eliminated from the study.

Statistical Measurement

The statistical measures of association used were determined by the hypotheses and the goals of the research problem. Statistical tests employed in the analysis of the data were (1) a test of significance based upon phi squared, (2) percentage distribution, and (3) percentage difference. In addition, chi squared was reported although probability is not relevant in a nonrandom sample, but acceptance of the phi coefficient is functionally related. As stated above, the test of statistical significance used in this study was based upon the phi squared.

These data were compiled from F.B.I. clearance records and corroborated by responses to items requesting this information in the administered questionnaire. A high consistency between official records and data supplied by the inmates was observed. This consistency supports the accuracy and reliability of the data.

Characteristics of the Data

Certain background data were tabulated from the questionnaire responses of the sample population, as well as from official sources.

1. Age. The distribution of age was from 18 through 64 years. The mean age was 29.8 years, and the median was 28.8 years (See Table 16, Appendix B).

2. <u>Race</u>. The data were comprised of 67.5 per cent White; 25.0 per cent Negroes; 5.5 per cent American Indian, and 2.0 per cent other (See Table 17, Appendix B). In terms of Wisconsin population which was 1.8 per cent Negroe (1960), the institutional data were definitely over-represented by Negroes. Approximately 52 per cent of the inmate population was from the metropolitan area of Milwaukee. Generally, Negroes in the Midwest population are characterized as an urban group. Even though Negroes make up 8.4 per cent of the Milwaukee population (1960), it is still clear that they were over-represented in the data.

3. <u>Formal Education Level Attained</u>. The range of formal education in the population studied was from the sixth grade through two years beyond a high school diploma. An unusually large number had graduated from high school and had further training beyond. Almost 38 per cent were in these two categories which would skew the measures of central tendency. The inmates' formal education mean was 10.5 years and the median was 11.4 (See Table 18, Appendix B).

In summation, the characteristics of the data appear similar to the total institution population. Although females in general have more formal education than most males in prison population, usually they are not this high. Also, an over-representation of Negroes is somewhat expected as they frequently come from densely populated urban areas.

4. <u>Criminal Offenses of the Study Data</u>. The types of crimes female committed display a wide diversity of criminal offenses. Some 29

different types of offenses indicate the variability of the criminal acts resulting in incarceration. Table 19, Appendix B, indicates some of the most frequent crimes committed by these female criminals: Forgery and Bad Checks (21.0 per cent), Sex Offenses (13.3 per cent), Murder (8.6 per cent), Theft (8.6 per cent and Prostitution (8.6 per cent). In contrast, some of the least frequent crimes committed were Arson, Auto Theft, Disorderly Conduct and Non-Support (See Table 20, Appendix B).

Some criminologists have argued that as criminals pass through life their criminal activity wanes in later years; it is often pointed out that the majority of adult offenders arrested and convicted are between eighteen and twenty-four and show a rapid decline after thirty-five. In other words, many law-breakers appear to "burn out." Tables 21 and 22, Appendix B, present a similar pattern of convictions and commitments with age of those females studied. The data were confirmed with records (89 inmates) which reveal that over 97 per cent of females have served time on one or more previous felonies (while only 2.3 per cent have never been sentenced to a correctional institution for a felony). A progression of crime with age is apparent, of course, since the inmate can only be convicted of a limited number of crimes and serves at least part of the sentences before she has an opportunity to commit more crimes. In addition, these data support the theory of progression into crime.

Findings

The empirical test generally substantiated the hypotheses of this study. A summation of these findings follows:

1. Those female inmates who perceived themselves as criminal
    tended to have referent groups who viewed them as criminal.
    These reference groups are referred to as negative referents
    or criminal referents.

2. Those female inmates who did not conceive of themselves as
    criminal tended to perceive their reference category as non-
    criminal.

3. Those female inmates who had committed a serious crime (for
    this commitment) were likely to report themselves as criminal
    while those inmates who did not have a criminal self-conception
    but who had committed a serious crime tended not to have negative
    referents. It should be noted that negative referents appears
    to be more crucial to a criminal self-conception than the
    seriousness of the criminal act (Type of crime).

4. There is no clear indication that inmates who commit a serious
    crime (for their present offense) will have reference groups
    whom they think perceive of them as criminal. The data did not
    substantiate a relationship between serious crime and negative
    reference. Further analysis of the data, however, reveals inmates
    with two or more previous felonies were more likely to have
    negative referents. It would appear that certain criminal factors
    merge with present type of crime and it is not possible from the
    data to determine when in time negative reference occurs.

5. Those females who defined their criminal acts as serious tended
    to perceive themselves as criminal while those women who also

defined their crime less serious were not likely to consider themselves as criminal.

6. Those inmates who at the time of the study had a criminal self-conception tended to have a criminal self-conception on arrival in the penal institution. It also was substantiated that inmates who did not perceive themselves as criminals at the time of measurement were not likely to have had a criminal self-conception upon arrival. The data show that the females on admission who had committed a serious crime were more likely to retain a criminal self-conception than if they had committed a less serious crime. However, of female inmates at the time of measurement only fifty-five per cent (21 of 38) of those committing a serious crime retained a criminal self-conception compared to ninety-one per cent (21 of 23) who had committed a less serious crime and retained a non-criminal self-conception.

Retention of a criminal self-conception is not paramount but possibly shows the effects of the institution's rehabilitation program. Much greater concern should be given to those females who have never considered themselves as criminals. It would seem logical that if criminal behavior resulted in their being adjudicated as criminals and sentenced to a penal institution, it would generate some concept of self as criminal. According to differential identification theory there is an emulation of anti-social or criminal identity. However, there are no data available to test the female for positive behavioral identification. She may be impaired in her attempt to identify herself satisfactorily within the interpersonal networks of the larger society.

Of some concern is the problem of positive reference groups. In this study an effort was made to direct the inmate's attention toward negative influences through the directions given in the questionnaire. It is quite possible that positive referents may affect the results and diminish the validity of the test instrument. It is logical that negative referents can only exist through a standard of comparison or some positive referents.

In future studies of this nature, it would also seem appropriate in interrogating the inmate to respond to her positive referents.

Another obvious concern is that there is no way of knowing whether the inmate's list of referents groups is a true list of influential groups or a series of rationalizations to meet the demands of the research question. It would seem plausible that the investigation challenge an inmate's response if she should list no reference group that has affected her behavior. This does not indicate that there has been no actual reference group. This position is similar to Kuhn's that behind all human behavior there are some referents or reference group even though it may not be recognized by the inmate being measured. At this point it becomes extremely difficult to discriminate between attitude and referents group. From this perspective of reference group theory, it may be argued that reference group influence is present even though an individual may not be capable of recognizing his reference group.

Six statistically significant relationships were found between hypothesized variables and inmate self-conception.

Women prisoners who had a criminal self-conception had:

1. more negative referents,

2. more serious crime,

3. more define their crime as serious,

4. more perceived a criminal self-conception upon arrival
    in prison.

On the other hand, those female inmates who did not perceive themselves as criminal had:

1. fewer negative referents,

2. more, less serious crime,

3. more perceive a non-criminal category,

4. more defined their crime as less serious,

5. more perceived themselves as non-criminal on arrival.

Other studies of this nature, preferably with more heterogenous populations and questionnaire of greater sensitivity, are needed in order to validate these findings.

Limitations of Study and Suggestions for Future Research

There are various limitations in this research. The need for more resources and time are always present in this type of study. In order to be more precise in the development of the criminal self-conception, the importance of measuring and controlling variables in the time order of occurrence is crucial. Several areas of influence might be considered. For example, there is the question of the process of incarceration which may be harsh as to its effect on the self-conception. Does total dependence upon the institution (institutionalization) have deleterious effects upon the inmate's self-conception? What about the inmate's environment that produced or at least encouraged the criminal act? What are the effects of deprivation of heterosexual relationships on the self-conception?

Another essential component of the inmate's self-conception is her status as a female. Finally there is the need to control previous criminal convictions and prison experiences which would permit a more accurate time order.

Future Study

It is also important that further research and scientific study be continued in order to provide a more complete understanding of the female inmate's criminal self-conception.

The following suggestions appear to be the most fruitful areas for further scientific research. First, the inmate's definition of a criminal should be refined so that a clear conceptualization of the developmental process is known. Second, attention should be extended to pre-institutional or background factors as to exposure and effect upon the development of a criminal self. Thirdly, consideration of other areas in which functional application of a criminal self-conception might be profitable in the relationship between probation and parole. That is, how does a criminal self-conception affect the successful rehabilitation compared with various types of treatment programs? Finally, it is suggested that research be done concerning the younger female (adolescent) in the developmental process, if possible, to determine if at onset of crime the criminal self-conception develops or at what point in a longitudinal process the self can be identified as criminal.

Contributions

This research has made several contributions to both differential identification theory and its possible application.

First of these contributions is the emphasis on the application of control variable to determine selective effects of reference group influence. The selected homogenous prison volunteers employed in this study provided data on the relationship between negative reference groups and criminal self-conception while other selected factors relating to criminal self-conception were held constant.

A second contribution made by this study is its elaboration of the theoretical positions of Sutherland and Glaser. Both of these authors have discussed some aspect of the question of criminal identities through reference groups and significant others affecting or impinging on a particular type of criminal behavior. The present findings have demonstrated that a criminal self-conception can be isolated in reference group research. The use of negative (criminal) referent opens the possibility to research on specific groups influencing a particular segment of the inmate's life.

The present study has not provided a means of evaluating proportional degrees of influence; however, it has measured a resultant influence.

In conclusion, the main contribution of this study is that an inmate's self-conception was found to be associated with the interpretation of significant others who had negative referents for her criminal actions. This differential self perception is believed to develop, in part, from interaction and reactions to significant others.

BIBLIOGRAPHY

LIST OF REFERENCES

Abrahamsen, David.
  1960   The Psychology of Crime. New York: Science Editions, page 126.

Becker, Howard S.
  1963   Outsiders. New York: The Free Press, page 9.

Blalock, Hubert.
  1960   Social Statistics. New York: McGraw-Hill Book Co., page 270.

Caldwell, Robert G.
  1956   Criminology. New York: The Ronald Press, pages 112-117, 182-185,
          186.

Caldwell, Robert G.
  1965   Criminology, (2nd Edition). New York: The Ronald Press,
          pages 199-200.

Clark, William L., and Marshall, William L.
  1952   A Treatise on the Law of Crimes, (5th Edition). Chicago: Callaghan
          and Company, pages 1-16.

Cressey, Donald R., and Ward, David A.
  1969   Delinquency, Crime, and Social Process. New York: Harper & Row,
          Publishers, pages 608-612.

Cressey, Donald R., and Sutherland, E. H.
  1960   Principles of Criminology, (6th Edition). Philadelphia:
          J. B. Lippincott Company, page 75.

Cressey, Donald R.
  1961   "Crime." Pages 21-76 in R. K. Merton and R. A. Nisbet (Editors),
          Contemporary Social Problems. Harcourt, Brace, and World,
          Incorporated.

Cressey, Donald R., and Sutherland, E. H.
  1970   Criminology, (8th Edition). Philadelphia: J. B. Lippincott
          Company, pages 126-131.

Ehrlich, Howard J.
   1969   "Attitudes, Behavior, and the Intervening Variables." The
          American Sociologist, American Sociological Association, Volume 4,
          No. 1, February, page 33.

Games, Paul A., and Klare, George R.
   1967   Elementary Statistics: Data Analysis for the Behavioral Sciences.
          New York: McGraw-Hill Book Company, page 515.

Giallombardo, Rose.
   1966   Society of Women. New York: John Wiley & Sons, Inc., Pages 2, 18.

Glaser, Daniel.
   1956   "Criminality Theories and Behavioral Images." American Journal
          of Sociology, Volume 61, No. 5, page 440.

Glueck, Sheldon and Eleanor.
   1934   Five Hundred Delinquent Women. New York: Alfred A. Knopf,
          Incorporated, page 288.

Guilford, V. P.
   1965   Fundamental Statistics in Psychology and Education, (4th Edition).
          New York: McGraw-Hill Book Company, page 334.

Hartung, Frank E.
   1966   Crime, Law and Society. Detroit: Wayne State Univ. Press.

Haskell, Martin R., and Yablonsky, Lewis.
   1970   Crime and Delinquency. Chicago: Rand McNally & Company,
          pages 60-64.

Hickman, Addison C., and Kuhn, Manford H.
   1956   Individuals, Groups and Economic Behavior. New York: The Dryden
          Press, pages 3-49, 208.

Hyman, Herbert H., and Sheatsley, Paul B.
   1954   "The Authoritarian Personality--A Methodological Critique."
          Pages 50-123 in Richard Christie and Marie Jahoda (Editors), Studies
          in the Scope and Method of "The Authoritarian Personality."
          Glencoe, Illinois: Free Press.

Kay, Barbara A.
   1961   "Differential Self Perceptions of Female Offenders." Unpublished
          Ph.D. Dissertation, The Ohio State University, page 46.

Knudten, Richard D.
   1970   Crime in a Complex Society. Homewood: The Dorsey Press, page 176.

Kuhn, Manford H., and McPartland, Thomas M.
   1954   "An Empirical Investigation of Self Attitudes." American
          Sociological Review, February, pages 68-75.

Lombroso, Cesare and Ferrero, William.
   1916   The Female Offender. New York and London: D. Appleton & Co.

Miller, D. E.
   1957   "Self Attitude and Political Roles: A Study in Role Taking
          Ability." Unpublished Master's Thesis, State University of Iowa,
          page 3.

Mueller, John H., and Schusseler, Karl F.
   1961   Statistical Reasoning in Sociology. Boston: Houghton, Mifflin
          Company, page 264.

Mulford, Harold A.
   1953   "Toward An Instrument to Measure the Self, Significant Others and
          Alcohol in the Symbolic Environment." Unpublished Ph.D. Dissertation,
          State University of Iowa.

Nardini, William.
   1958   "Criminal Self Conceptions in the Penal Community: An Empirical
          Study." Unpublished Ph.D. Dissertation, State University of Iowa,
          pages 101, 121, 136-138.

National Prisoner Statistics.
   1962   "Prisoners in the State and Federal Institutions 1960." United
          States Department of Justice, Robert F. Kennedy, Attorney General,
          J. V. Bennett, Director, September. Washington 25, D.C.

Newcomb, Theodore.
   1950   Social Psychology. New York: Dryden Press, pages 225-226.

Pollak, Otto.
   1950   The Criminality of Women. Philadelphia: University of Pennsylvania
          Press, pages 1-7, 44-45, 154-155.

Payak, Bertha J.
   1963   "Understanding the Female Offender." Federal Probation, Volume 27,
          No. 4 (December).

Reckless, Walter C., and Murray, E.
   1956   "Self Concept as an Insulator Against Delinquency." American
          Sociological Review, Volume 21, December, pages 744-746.

Reckless, Walter C., Dimitz, S., and Kay, Barbara.
  1957   "Self Concept in Potential Delinquency and Non-Delinquency."
          American Sociological Review, Volume 22, October, pages 566-590.

Reckless, Walter C.
  1961   The Crime Problem, (3rd Edition). Appleton-Century-Crofts,
          Incorporated, pages 78, 311.

Reckless, Walter C.
  1967   The Crime Problem, (4th Edition). Appleton-Century-Crofts,
          Incorporated, page 148.

Reiss, Albert, and Rhodes, Lewis.
  1964   "An Empirical Test of Differential Association Theory." Journal
          of Research in Crime and Delinquency, January, pages 5-18.

Rodgers, Carl.
  1951   Client-Centered Therapy: Its Current Practice, Implications, and
          Theory. Boston: Houghton, Mifflin Company.

Rose, Arnold M.
  1962   Human Behavior and Social Process. Boston: Houghton, Mifflin
          Company, page 3.

Schur, Edwin M.
  1969   Our Criminal Society: The Social and Legal Sources of Crime in
          America. Englewood Cliffs: Prentice-Hall, Inc., pages 115-118.

Shibutani, Tamotsu.
  1961   Society and Personality: An Interactionist Approach to Social
          Psychology. Englewood Cliffs, New Jersey: Prentice-Hall,
          Incorporated, page 261.

Sutherland, E. H.
  1939   Principles of Criminology. Philadelphia: J. B. Lippincott Company,
          pages 4-9.

Sutherland, E. H.
  1955   Principles of Criminology, (5th Edition). Philadelphia:
          J. B. Lippincott Company, pages 77-80.

Tappan, P. W.
  1947   "Who is the Criminal?" American Sociological Review, Volume 12,
          February, page 100.

Thomas, William I.
  1923   The Unadjusted Girl. Boston: Little, Brown, & Company,
          pages 1-69.

Thomas W. I., and Thomas, D. S.
  1928   <u>The Child in America</u>. New York: Alfred A. Knopf, Incorporated,
         page 572.

<u>Crime in the United States</u>
  1970   "Uniform Crime Reports - 1969." Washington, D.C.: U.S.
         Government Printing Office, page 111.

Walker, Helen M., and Lev, Joseph.
  1953   <u>Statistical Inference</u>. New York: Holt, Rinehard and Winston,
         page 106.

Ward, David., and Kasselbaum, Gene.
  1965   <u>Women's Prison</u>. Chicago: Aldine Publishing Company, V-X.

Winch, Robert F., and Campbell, Donald T.
  1969   "Proof? No. Evidence? Yes. The Significance of Tests of
         Significance." <u>American Sociologist 4</u> (May, 1969): pages 140-143.

Wrong, Denis H.
  1961   "The Oversocialized Conception of Man in Modern Sociology."
         <u>American Sociological Review</u>, XXVI (April, 1961), pages 183-193.

GENERAL REFERENCES

Clinard, Marshall B.
  1957   Sociology of Deviant Behavior. New York: Rinehard and Company,
         Incorporated.

Cressey, Donald R.
  1961   The Prison: Studies in Institutional Organization and Change.
         New York: Henry Holt and Company.

Glaser, Daniel.
  1960   "Differential Association and Criminological Prediction." Social
         Problems, Volume 7 (Summer), pages 2-6.

Goffman, Erving.
  1961   Asylums Essays on the Social Situation of Mental and Their
         Inmates. Garden City, New York: Doubleday and Company,
         Incorporated.

Greenwald, Dr. Harold.
  1958   The Call Girl. New York: Ballantine Books.

Harris, Sara.
  1958   Nobody Cries for Me. New York: The New American Library, A Signet
         Book.

Hyman, Herbert H.
  1942   "The Psychology of Status." Archives of Psychology, No. 269.

Hyman, Herbert H.
  1955   Survey Design and Analyses. Glencoe, Illinois: The Free Press.

Johoda, Marie, and Cook, S. W.
  1954   Research Methods in Social Relations. New York: The Dryden Press.

Kuhn, Manford H.
  1964a "The Reference Group Reconsidered." The Sociological Quarterly,
         Volume 5, No. 1, pages 5-21.

Kuhn, Manford H.
  1964b "Major Trends in Symbolic Interaction Theory in the Past Twenty-Five
         Years." The Sociological Quarterly, Volume 5, No. 1, Pages 61-84.

Lindesmith, Alfred R. and Strauss, Anslem L.
  1954   Social Psychology. New York: Dryden Press.

Mead, George H.
  1934   Mind Self and Society. Charles W. Morris (Editor). Chicago:
          University of Chicago Press.

Murtagh, John M. and Harris, Sara.
  1955   Cast the First Stone. New York: The New American Library,
          A Signet Book.

Palmer, Neil M.
  1954   "The Relation of Selected Variables: The Use of Membership Group
          as REference Group." Unpublished Ph.D. Dissertation, State
          University of Iowa.

Phillips, Bernard S.
  1966   Social Research/Strategy and Tactics. New York: The Macmillan
          Company.

Riley, Matilda White.
  1963   Sociological Research. New York: Harcourt, Brace and World,
          Incorporated.

Sarbin, Theodore R.
  1954   "Role Theory," Gardner, Lindzey (Editor). Cambridge, Massachusetts:
          Westley Publishing Company, Incorporated.

Sherif, Muzafer, and Cantril, Hadley.
  1947   The Psychology of Ego-Involvements. New York: John Wiley and
          Sons, Incorporated.

Sherif, Muzafer, and Corolyn W.
  1953a   Groups in Harmony and Tension. New York: Harper & Row, Publishers,
          Incorporated.

Sherif, Muzafer, and Wilson, M. O. (Editors).
  1953b   Group Relations at the Crossroads. New York: Harper & Bros.

Shibutani, Tamotsu.
  1955   "Reference Groups as Perspectives." American Journal of Sociology,
          Volume 60, May, pages 562-569.

Sutherland, Edwin H.
  1947   Principles of Criminology. New York: J. B. Lippincott Company.

United States Census of Population.
  1960   United States Department of Commerce, Bureau of Census,
          Washington, D.C.

Vold, George B.
  1958   Theoretical Criminology. Oxford University Press.

Waisanen, Fredrick.
  1954   "The Prejudice Variable: A Social Psychological and Methodological
          Study." Unpublished Ph.D. Dissertation, State University of Iowa.

Wolfgane, Marvin.
  1962   The Sociology of Crime and Delinquency. New York: John Wiley
          & Sons, Incorporated, pages 28-34.

Zelditch, Morris.
  1959   A Basic Course in Sociological Statistics. New York: Henry Holt
          and Company.

APPENDIX A

QUESTIONNAIRE

INTRODUCTION TO QUESTIONS

In cooperation with the State University of Iowa, a study of penal institutions in being made. Your answers to the questions herein asked will be most helpful.

As this is a research project, and not a regular part of the program here, your answers will <u>not</u> affect your relationship with this institution in any way. This information is strictly confidential.

DO NOT OPEN BOOKLET UNTIL TOLD TO DO SO

Part 1 (A)

There are twenty numbered blanks on the page below. Please write twenty answers to this simple question "WHO AM I?" in these blanks. Just give twenty different answers to this question. Answer as if you were giving the answer to yourself, not to somebody else. Write your answers in the order that they occur to you. Don't worry about logic or "importance." Go along fairly fast: the time for this part of the questionnaire is limited.

WHO AM I

1. _____
2. _____
3. _____
4. _____
5. _____
6. _____
7. _____
8. _____
9. _____
10. _____
11. _____
12. _____
13. _____
14. _____
15. _____
16. _____
17. _____
18. _____
19. _____
20. _____

STOP! (Do not go on until told to do so)

Part (1)

1. How old are you?

    Put your age here: _____

2. Where were you born?

    Check one of the following:

    Farm   _____

    Small town   _____

    Small city   _____

    Large city   _____

3. How many brothers and sisters are there in your family?

    Number of sisters _____

    Number of brothers _____

4. Do you think that you received a fair trial before you were convicted and sent to prison?

    YES _____   NO _____

5. Would you say that you are guilty of the crime for which you were convicted?

    YES _____   NO _____

STOP! (Do not go on until told to do so)

Part (2)

Below is a list of statements about what a criminal is. For each of the following statements indicate whether you personally would or would not make this statement about a criminal.

I would say that a criminal is: YES   NO

1. A person who breaks the criminal law.........   ____   ____

2. A person who often breaks the criminal law....   ____   ____

3. A person who commits a serious crime (such
    as murder, robbery, etc.)....................   ____   ____

4. A person who serves more time in prison than
    out of prison................................   ____   ____

5. A person who intends to commit a wrong........   ____   ____

6. A person who would cheat his best friend......   ____   ____

7. A person who has no respect for law and order.   ____   ____

(PLEASE GO ON TO THE NEXT PAGE)

Part (3)

In the numbered blanks below, please list those groups or people whose opinions or judgments of you and your behavior you consider important. (Do not give proper names. Simply specify their relationship or connection to you.)

1. _____

2. _____

3. _____

4. _____

5. _____

6. _____

7. _____

8. _____

9. _____

10. _____

(PLEASE GO ON TO NEXT PAGE)

Part (4)

In the numbered blanks below please list those groups or people who think of you as a criminal. (Do not give proper names. Simply specify their relationship or connection with you.)

1. _____

2. _____

3. _____

4. _____

5. _____

6. _____

7. _____

8. _____

9. _____

10. _____

(PLEASE GO ON TO THE NEXT PAGE)

Part (5)

Which of the following individuals would you say think of you as
a criminal?

	YES	NO
Guards.................	____	____
Shop supervisors.......	____	____
Other inmates.........	____	____
An inmate friend.......	____	____
The social worker......	____	____

Part (6)

Which of the following individuals would you say think of you as
a criminal? (In the event you do <u>not</u> have a brother, sister, spouse, etc.,
write NONE.)

	YES	NO
1. Mother...........	____	____
2. Father...........	____	____
3. Brother..........	____	____
4. Sister...........	____	____
5. Son..............	____	____
6. Daughter.........	____	____
7. Uncle............	____	____
8. Aunt.............	____	____
9. Cousin...........	____	____

(PLEASE GO ON TO THE NEXT PAGE)

	YES	NO

1. Have you ever thought of yourself as a criminal?   ____ ____

2. If you answered "YES" to the above question, at what age in your lifetime did you first come to think of yourself as a criminal?

    Put the age here ____

3. How old were you when you first received a police record?

    Put the age here ____

4. For what kind of offense did you receive your <u>first</u> police record?

    Put kind of offense here _____

	YES	NO

5. Did you think of yourself as a criminal when you were first arrested by the police for this offense?   ____ ____

6. Did you think of yourself as a criminal <u>after</u> arrest but while in <u>jail</u> <u>awaiting</u> trial for this offense?   ____ ____

7. Did you think of yourself as a criminal when you were being <u>tried</u> before the <u>court</u> for this offense?   ____ ____

8. Did you think of yourself as a criminal when you <u>first</u> came here to this prison?   ____ ____

9. Have you ever thought of yourself as a criminal at <u>any</u> <u>time</u> <u>other</u> <u>than</u> <u>those</u> <u>times</u> mentioned in the above questions?   ____ ____

10. If you said "YES" to question 9 explain below at what <u>other</u> <u>time</u> in your life you thought of yourself as a criminal.   ____ ____

(PLEASE GO ON TO THE NEXT PAGE)

Part 8

YES   NO

1. Do you know of any person on the outside who has committed as serious, or more serious a crime than you have, who was either set free or was given less of a sentence than yours?

                                                          ____   ____

2. Would you say that there are many people who have committed just as serious a crime as you have who were either set free or given less of a sentence than you?

    ____   ____

3. Would you say that there are many people who have committed a more serious crime than you have who were either set free or given less of a sentence than you?

    ____   ____

4. Do you now think of yourself as a criminal?

    ____   ____

5. How did you please at your trial?   Guilty _____   Not Guilty _____

Part (9)

1. For what length of time is your present sentence? (That is, for what length of time have you been sentenced?)

                                Put number of years here _____

2. On what month, day, and year did you come to this prison?

    Month _____   Day _____   Year _____

3. How much schooling have you completed?

    Grade school _____   High School _____

    College _____   Professional School _____

4. What is your present marital status?

    Single _____   Separated _____

    Married _____   Widow _____

    Divorced _____

(PLEASE GO ON TO THE NEXT PAGE)

Part (10)

5. For what kind of offense are you now serving time?
   (Check one of the following.)

   Murder .... _____

   Assault with intent to murder......................... _____

   Involuntary manslaughter .... _____

   Assault with intent to commit great bodily injury .... _____

   Robbery .... _____

   Robbery with aggravation .... _____

   Intent to commit robbery .... _____

   Prostitution and commercialized vice .... _____

   Burglary .... _____

   Burglary with aggravation .... _____

   Larceny .... _____

   Breaking and entering .... _____

   Forgery .... _____

   False drawing or uttering of checks .... _____

   Operating a motor vehicle while intoxicated .... _____

6. If you have committed an offense <u>not</u> listed above please write it in this
   space:
   _____

Part (11)

List your three best friends: 1._____

                              2._____

                              3._____

(PLEASE GO ON TO THE NEXT PAGE)

97

Part (11 cont'd.)

Now, list your three best friends in this institution:

1._____

2._____

3._____

Part (12)

		YES	NO
1.	Have you ever told a lie?	____	____
2.	Have you ever gossiped?	____	____
3.	Have you ever cheated?	____	____
4.	Have you ever had a fight with a good friend?	____	____
5.	Have you ever become angry with your parents?	____	____
6.	Have you ever taken anything that did not belong to you?	____	____

STOP! PLEASE TURN IN THIS QUESTIONNAIRE.

TABLES

TABLE 16

AGE OF STUDY POPULATION OF WISCONSIN HOME
FOR WOMEN

Age	Number	Per Cent	Cumulative Per Cent
50 and over	5	4.8	100.0
45-49	4	3.8	95.2
40-44	9	8.6	91.4
35-39	10	9.5	82.8
30-34	20	19.0	73.3
25-29	19	18.1	54.3
20-24	26	24.8	36.2
19 and under	12	11.4	11.4
TOTAL	105	100.0	100.0

Mean = 29.76
Median = 28.81

TABLE 17

RACIAL COMPOSITION OF STUDY POPULATION
OF WISCONSIN HOME FOR WOMEN

Race	Number	Per Cent
White	71	67.6
Negro	26	24.8
American Indian	6	5.7
Other	2	1.9
TOTAL	105	100.0

See Statistical Abstract of the United States, 1967 (88th Ed)
Washington, D.C.; U. S. Department of Commerce, U. S. Government
Printing Office.

TABLE 18

GRADE LEVEL ATTAINED THROUGH FORMAL EDUCATION
OF STUDY POPULATION FOR WISCONSIN HOME FOR WOMEN

Grade-Level	Number	Per Cent	Cumulative Per Cent
13 +	13	12.5	100.0
12	26	25.0	77.5
11	22	21.0	62.5
10	16	15.5	41.5
9	10	9.5	26.0
8	15	14.5	16.5
7	1	1.0	2.0
6	1	1.0	1.0
TOTAL	104	100.0	100.0

Mean = 10.51
Median - 11.39

TABLE 19

TYPES OF OFFENSES FOR WHICH FEMALE INMATES
IN THE STUDY POPULATION WERE COMMITTED

Offense	Number	Per Cent
Murder *	9	8.6
Manslaughter *	4	3.8
Robbery *	6	5.7
Assault *	4	3.8
Burglary *	4	3.8
Theft Except Auto *	9	8.6
Auto Theft	1	1.0
Fraud or Embezzlement *	4	3.8
Forgery or False Checks	22	21.0
Prostitution	9	8.6
Other Sex Offenses *	14	13.3
Narcotics *	4	3.8
Non-Support	2	1.9
Disorderly Conduct	1	1.0
All Other	12	11.4
TOTAL	105	100.1

* Offenses were considered as serious crimes.

TABLE 20

TYPOLOGY OF OFFENSES[1] FOR WHICH THE FEMALE
POPULATION WAS COMMITTED FOR PRESENT INCARCERATION

Offense	Number	Per Cent
Crimes of Violence[2]	17	16.2
Sex Offenses	23	21.9
Robbery	6	5.7
Burglary	4	3.8
Auto Theft	1	1.0
Larceny (Fraud)	13	12.4
Forgery[3]	22	21.0
Non-Support[4]	2	1.9
Narcotics	4	3.8
Other	13	12.4
TOTAL	105	100.1

[1]This 10 category typology of offenses is utilized here for comparative purposes. The typology was suggested by: Alfred R. Lindesmith and H. Warren Dunham, "Some Principles of Criminal Typology," Social Forces, Volume 19, No. 3, March, 1941, pp. 307-314.

[2]This category included murder, manslaughter, attempts to kill and wound, and all assaults.

[3]This category included all check offenses.

[4]Non-support is equated for abuse for females.

TABLE 21

NUMBER OF PREVIOUS FELONIES COMMITTED BY THE
STUDY POPULATION (NOT INCLUDING PRESENT COMMITMENT)

Number of Felonies	Number	Per Cent	Cumulative Per Cent
8	1	1.1	100.0
7	2	2.2	98.9
6	4	4.3	96.7
5	6	6.5	92.4
4	14	15.2	85.9
3	14	15.2	70.7
2	17	18.5	55.5
1	27	29.4	37.0
0	7	7.6	7.6
TOTAL	92	100.0	100.0

Mean = 2.55
Median = 2.27

TABLE 22

PREVIOUS FELONIES AND AGE OF FEMALE INMATES OF STUDY
POPULATION AT WISCONSIN HOME FOR WOMEN

Previous Felonies	Age	Number of Inmates	Per Cent	Cumulative Per Cent
0	under 18	2	2.3	2.3
1	19-22	22	24.7	27.0
2	23-29	20	22.5	49.5
3	30-34	18	20.2	69.7
4+	35+	27	30.3	100.0
TOTAL		89	100.0	100.0

Eighty-nine of the ninety-two previous felonies correlates age
with previous felons. If these data are accurate the theory of
progression into crime is supported.

TABLE 23

NEGATIVE REFERENCE GROUPS[1]

	None		Other Inmates and Inmate Friends		Inmate Friends, other Inmates and Non-Penal Significant Others		Total
	N		N		N		Total
Criminal Self-Conception	2	(10)	7	(6)	17	(10)	26
Non-Criminal Self-Conception	46	(38)	21	(22)	35	(42)	102
TOTAL	48		28		52		128

Chi square: x^2 = 16.74, 2 d.f., p < .001

[1]William Nardini, "Criminal Self-Conceptions in The Penal Community: An Empirical Study," unpublished doctoral dissertation, State University of Iowa, 1958, p. 63.